# THE
# UNIQUELY
# ME
# BOOK

## it's a God thing!

D1040397

# Other Books in the Young Women of Faith Library

# THE UNIQUELY ME BOOK

## it's a God thing!

Written by Nancy Rue
Illustrated by Lyn Boyer

Zonderkidz

# Zonder**kidz**.

*The children's group of Zondervan*

www.zonderkidz.com

*The Uniquely Me Book*
Copyright © 2002 by Women of Faith

Requests for information should be addressed to:

Zonderkidz, *Grand Rapids, Michigan 49530*

ISBN: 0–310–70248–8

All Scripture quotations, unless otherwise indicated, are taken from the HOLY BIBLE, NEW INTERNA-TIONAL VERSION ®. Copyright © 1973, 1978, 1984 by International Bible Society. Used by permission of Zondervan. All Rights Reserved.

All rights reserved. No part of this publication may be reproduced, stored in a retrieval system, or trans-mitted in any form or by any means — electronic, mechanical, photocopy, recording, or any other — except for brief quotations in printed reviews, without the prior permission of the publisher.

Zonderkidz is a trademark of Zondervan.

Published in association with the literary agency of Alive Communications, Inc., 7680 Goddard Street, Suite 200, Colorado Springs, CO 80920.

*Editor: Barbara J. Scott*
*Interior design: Michelle Lenger*
*Art direction: Michelle Lenger*
*Printed in the United States of America*

03 04 05  06  07 08/❖ DC/11 10 9 8 7 6 5 4 3 2

# Contents

# I Don't Have Gifts, Do I?

There are different kinds of gifts, but the same Spirit.
There are different kinds of service, but the same Lord.
There are different kinds of working,
but the same God works all of them in all men.

*1 Corinthians 12:4–6*

When **Lily, Suzy,** and **Reni** were in elementary school, they were all invited into the "gifted program." As their friend **Zooey** put it, that seemed to mean they were "way smarter than the rest of us kids." Every time Zooey watched them leave the regular classroom to go do some special activity, she would slump down in her desk and think, *I wish I were gifted.*

So when Lily, Suzy, and Reni took Zooey to church with them, and the Sunday school teacher started talking about the "spiritual gifts" people have, Zooey groaned and thought, *Here we go again. I'm gonna be in the UN-gifted group.*

But the teacher made it sound like *everybody* had at least one spiritual gift. Zooey couldn't help it—she had to raise her hand and set this lady straight.

"I'm not gifted," Zooey told her. "I'm in the dumb group."

That's when the teacher set *Zooey* straight. The gifts she was talking about were nothing like that special, "only-certain-people-get-invited" program at school. When it came to these gifts:

- Everybody has one or more.
- The gifts don't have anything to do with how smart you are or how talented or pretty or rich.
- They aren't the kind that make *you* special—they are supposed to be used to help the body of Christ—the church—grow and be more and more wonderful.

That was all Zooey had to hear. She was ready to find out what her gifts were and go for it!

How about you? Do you want to know what these gifts are? Would you like to find out which ones God put in the "you" package before you were born *and* learn how you can use them? If so, this is the book for you. It comes with a warning label, though:

READING THIS BOOK MAY CAUSE
EXCITEMENT, **JOY,** AND SUDDEN BURSTS OF ENERGY!

If you can handle that, you're ready to begin. Let's start with what God says about this whole spiritual gifts thing.

## HOW IS THIS A God Thing?

In the very early days of the Christian church—*way* back before there were church buildings with steeples and congregations with pastors or even youth programs or choirs—Paul wrote letters to the various groups of Christians, telling them what he was learning from God about how they should live together. He told the people of Corinth, for example, that each one of them had something *important* to contribute to the life of their Christian community. He called those something-important things *spiritual gifts*.

People being human the way they are, the fussing and arguing started right away.

"I can speak in tongues, which is a whole lot more important than you just teaching a class."

"Oh, yeah? You don't have the gift of prophecy, so don't go thinking you're all that!"

So Paul had to set them straight. He said, "There are different kinds of gifts, but the same Spirit. There are different kinds of service, but the same Lord. There are different kinds of working, but the same God works all of them in all men" (1 Corinthians 12:4–6).

Each person's gifts were special, because each person's gifts had come from the same place—God. Not only that, but each person's gifts had to be used for the whole community, or the whole community was going to fall apart.

Just to make sure they understood that, Paul used the human body as an example. He said, "The body is a unit, though it is made up of many parts" (1 Corinthians 12:12). You've got your feet, your hands, your ears, and your eyes, and each one of them has its own job to do. Paul said, "If the whole body were an eye, where would the sense of hearing be? If the whole body were an ear, where would the sense of smell be?" (1 Corinthians 12:17).

About that time, the people of Corinth probably were starting to feel pretty lame about competing with each other over their gifts, but just in case they were tempted to go at it again, Paul wrote, "God has arranged the parts in the body, every one of them, just as he wanted them to be" (1 Corinthians 12:18).

So what were these gifts Paul was talking about? There are several lists of spiritual gifts in the New Testament, but we'll be talking about just the ones that you're likely to find in yourself right now. Later in your life, you may discover God-given gifts for use in the church that will mature as you do—so we'll leave those for you to read about when the time comes. There definitely are gifts you can use and develop now, even if you're as young as eight years old. They're given different names in the Bible, but to make sure they're easy for you to understand, we're going to call them:

- *Speaking Gifts*—teacher, encourager, perceiver
- *Serving Gifts*—server, giver, compassion child
- *Gifts that Involve Speaking and Serving*—leader, administrator

As we go along, we'll explain what each of these gifts is, and you'll be able to see which ones best describe you. Before you do that, though, you need to know one other very important thing the New Testament tells us: "Each one should use whatever gift he has received to serve others, faithfully administering God's grace in its various forms" (1 Peter 4:10).

For you, that means *two* very important things:

1. The gifts we're talking about are not the kind you keep to yourself or show to just a few close friends. Spiritual gifts are given to you by God to be used in the Christian community to help it grow. Being able to juggle four raw eggs without dropping a single one may be a gift, but it isn't a spiritual gift. You might use that gift once in a while to entertain your youth group or get all the toddlers in the church nursery to stop wailing, but every church doesn't have to have an egg juggler. Every church *does,* however, need people who teach, encourage, and just seem to know how others are feeling. Every church needs servers, givers, and people with compassion. And where would any church be without leaders and administrators? (If you don't know what some of those words mean, hang in there. We'll explain everything!)

2. Most books are meant to be read by yourself. This one is different! You'll get the most out of this book if you get a few of your friends to read it at the same time so you can do the **Just Do It** activities together. After all, we're talking about gifts you'll use all your life to serve a *group* of people. So why not learn about them and practice with them as a group? If you can't think of anyone who would join you, go ahead and read and enjoy it on your own, but pray and keep your eyes open. Bringing people together to do good stuff for him is one of God's best gifts!

You'll notice that when we talked about the spiritual gifts, we placed them into three groups:

- Speaking Gifts
- Serving Gifts
- Gifts that Involve Both Speaking and Serving

Before we talk in other chapters about exactly which gifts you have, let's find out which of the three groups your gifts fall into. You may find out that you have gifts in two or even all three of the categories—or you may see that all your gifts seem to cluster in one area. Just remember that whatever you discover, that's the way God wanted it when he created you. Finding your gifts will be like hearing God whisper one of his "you-secrets" right in your ear.

Each statement below has three possible endings. Put a check or a star next to *every* ending that is true for you. That means, in some cases, you might check more than one ending. Be *really* honest—don't check anything just because you think it's what you "should" do. (There are no "shoulds" in this quiz!)

If there is a group project to do, I like to

    a.   _____ show other people how to do it.

    b.   ✓ get in there and actually do the work.

    c.   _____ organize the whole thing.

If a room needs to be cleaned after the group project is done, I would

    a.   _____ say how it ought to be done.

    b.   ✓ get a broom and start sweeping.

    c.   ✓ figure out who could do what part of the cleanup. *and then start cleaning*

If a friend or brother or sister has a problem, I

    a.   ✓ give advice.

    b.   ✓ do something to make the situation better.

    c.   _____ go through the solution step-by-step.

If there's an argument among my friends (or a heated discussion!), I want to

    a.   ✓ give my opinion.

    b.   ✓ do something to stop it.

c. _____ help everybody see how it could be resolved.

I think I can help my friends when

a. ✓ they're confused about God things.

b. ✓ they're sad.

c. ✓ they have trouble getting along with people.

Often I

a. ✓ read a good book.

b. _____ make something with my hands.

c. _____ make lists of all the cool things I want to do.

When I'm upset I

a. ✓ keep other people from seeing how I feel.

b. ✓ show my feelings to other people.

c. _____ figure out who I should show my feelings to before I do it.

If my friends and I were going to put on a play, I would want to

a. ✓ act in it.

b. ✓ do the behind-the-scenes stuff (like costumes and makeup and scenery).

c. _____ come up with the ideas and direct it.

When it comes to making decisions, I

a. ✓ make them very quickly and easily.

b. _____ have a hard time deciding what to do.

c. ✓ do a lot of thinking before I decide, but when I do, it's easy.

I like to work with

a. _____ myself.

b. __✓__ one person at a time.

c. __✓__ a whole group of people.

Count the number of **a**'s, **b**'s, and **c**'s you checked and write the totals here:

"**a**" 4 5 3

"**b**" 6 5 5

"**c**" 2 2

Before we talk about what those numbers mean, remember this: No group of gifts is better or more important than any other group. The "body of Christ" needs toes as much as it needs lungs!

You might have a two-way or even a three-way tie, or high numbers in more than one group. That just means you have gifts in more than one area—so read all the ones that are about you.

**If you scored five or more in the "a" group,** you have some *Speaking Gifts.* That means that you have a gift for using the spoken word to teach people how to do things or understand hard stuff, to encourage people when they're bummed out or not sure of themselves, and to help people see what's right and what's wrong. You have no trouble saying what's on your mind. You're probably okay with speaking in front of a group of people, once you get over a small case of the jitters. *And when people need somebody to talk to, you're one of the first people they'll turn to.* Those are all gifts you can use to help keep the body of Christ on the right track.

**If you scored five or more in the "b" group,** you have some *Serving Gifts.* That means you would rather do than talk, work behind the scenes than be in the spotlight, show it than say it. You may have a gift for carrying out instructions, being generous, or knowing what other people need. You get a kick out of doing things to surprise or help people. You like to be the helper. And it's a pretty sure thing that you're already doing what needs to be done to solve a problem before most people even know there's a problem! Those are all gifts you can use to help keep the body of Christ running smoothly.

**If you scored five or more in the "c" group,** you have some *Gifts that Involve Both Speaking and Serving.* That means you are a natural leader or that you are good at planning and making sure the plans are carried out. You can get other people to do things without thinking you're too bossy. You not only have great ideas but you get things done. And there's no doubt that you know how to bring people together and get them working as a team. Those are all gifts you can use to help keep the body of Christ growing.

NOTE: Even though the chapters in this book are divided into the three kinds of gifts, read all of them, even if you think you have no gifts in a certain area. It's a good thing to understand all the gifts, just as it's important to understand your whole body.

# Girlz WANT TO KNOW

❀ *ZOOEY: I like this whole spiritual gifts thing. I just found out I'm a server, like, in a big way! But, see, I don't go to church. Do I still have gifts then? Can I still use them?*

You definitely still have your gifts, Zooey. They came with you, just like your gray eyes and great smile. And in some ways you can use them even if you don't belong to a church. As a server, you can be generous and compassionate with your own friends and family and do all kinds of wonderful things for them. But the best thing you can do for them is help them get closer to God, and before you can do that, you need to be close to God—and the place to learn to do that is in a church, which is just a Christian community. If your family doesn't want to go to a church, ask your friends who do belong to one if you can go with them. Then pray that the enthusiasm and the love and all the other good stuff you bring home with you will inspire the rest of your family to go with you. That's the best service of all!

*LILY: I love my gifts! I tied three ways, and I am so ready to go right to work in my church. But I know my mom and dad are going to say, "Slow down, Lily. You can't run the place yet!" How can I use my gifts if people think I'm just a kid?*

Kids are way important to the life of a church. People don't just wake up one day as adults and say, "Okay. Time to use my gifts. I'm a grown-up now." The kid years are really important for learning how to use those gifts— and you don't just learn by sitting around watching everybody else. You learn by doing. Look for the opportunities to do that are appropriate for your age group.

Since you have speaking gifts, can you volunteer to read out loud in your Sunday school class? Ask for parts in pageants and puppet shows that require learning a lot of lines? Look for chances to read to the preschoolers or help with

Vacation Bible School? When it comes to your serving gifts, you can really go for it when the Sunday school has a food drive, or you can be the first one on the bus when your class takes cookies to a nursing home. As for your speaking and serving gifts, think of some projects you would like to see the kids your age in the church do (like write letters to some of those folks you met at the nursing home), and present them to your teacher.

No, you won't be directing the entire choir or organizing a church supper for four hundred people, but what you can do is just as important—and there will be plenty of time for those four hundred-plate dinners later!

✿ *SUZY: I have a lot of serving gifts—at least, that's what the quiz said—but I'm way too shy to ever really do any of those things in my church. Do you think God is disappointed in me?*

God definitely understands where you're coming from. If you'll recall, he actually picked out shy people to do some mighty big jobs—like Moses, for example. Whatever gifts God has given you, he has also given you what it takes to use them. It may not feel like you can raise your hand and volunteer to take up the collection on Youth Sunday, but you can. It just takes a little praying and a lot of believing that God is right there beside you, giving you little tricks to help you along—things like, "What is the worst that can happen, Suzy? Dropping the collection plate? So what! You just pick it up and keep going! You'll be embarrassed? Oh, maybe for a few minutes, but both you and everybody else will forget before you know it. Just do it, Suzy— you're going to love it when you do."

Start with small things, like helping your Sunday school teacher pass out supplies or erasing the dry-erase board for her. Then maybe ask if you can bring snacks for next week's class (after you check with your mom, of course!). If you see that an older lady in the congregation looks lonely, make a drawing for her to hang on her refrigerator. Once you get started, there will be no stopping you!

✿ *KRESHA: I'm already using my serving gifts—I just didn't know it until I started reading this book! The problem is, when I get to play with the little kids in the nursery or pass out pieces of cake at a church din-*

*ner, I have so much fun. I feel really good about myself. But that's not why I'm supposed to be doing it, right?*

If you feel good when you do things for other people, you are absolutely using your gifts the way God wants you to! Joy is one of the best ways of telling that you're doing the right thing. If that were the only reason you did it—because it made you feel good—that would be a problem. But it sounds like you use your serving gifts to make other people happy, and your feelings of happiness just come along with it. Isn't it cool how that works?

# Just Do It

Ready to take the first step? Look at the steps listed below and choose the one that fits you best.

- If you don't have a church—a body of Christ—where you can use the gifts we're about to explore, make a list of the friends you have who do have a church and who sometimes talk about how much they love it there or how much fun it is to do stuff there. Then ask your parents for permission to ask one of your friends if you could go to church with her. If Mom and Dad give you the okay, do that. If you feel comfortable there, go on as many Sundays as you can. Start learning everything you can while you're there. If you have questions, ask your friend's parents. It's a good way to find a place where you can use your gifts.
- If you do have a church family, and you have close friends who don't, invite one or more of them to go to church with you. Make it a special event for your friend. Could she spend the night with you the night before? Could you make her a special card to welcome her? Be sure to stay with her the whole time, introducing her to people she doesn't know and making sure she knows what

to do (and where the bathroom is!). Make her feel as comfortable as you can—in your own special, gifted way.

If you're reading this book with friends—let's call that your "Gifts Group"—you can work together, each bringing a friend-without-a-church on the same Sunday. Make it special, as we've suggested above. It'll be a party!

# Talking to God About It

We're going to use the word "**TOY**" to help you pray in this book.

**T** is for *thanksgiving*.

**O** is for the things you'll want to ask for on behalf of *other* people.

**Y** is for the things you'll want to ask for just for *yourself*.

As you pray about your spiritual gifts—

- Thank God for the gifts you're discovering you have. Tell him why you're glad to have them.
- Ask God to help other people you know—by name—discover their gifts too.
- Ask God to help you learn how to use your gifts to make the body of Christ stronger, bigger, and better.
- Don't forget to give the strongest, biggest, best *amen* you can!

The best gift (of any kind) I ever gave anyone was . . .

helping someone
be really nice

When I helped and
stayed with one of my
best friends ~~Sara Maria~~
and helped her finish
going down the models
when everybody
else left.

# Speak Up!

**If anyone speaks, he should do it as one
speaking the very words of God.**
*1 Peter 4:11*

**L**ily definitely has a gift for speaking. She's the first to raise her hand in any class. She isn't afraid to express her opinion about—well—just about anything! Not only that, but she's good at explaining things, and she'll do it for twenty, maybe even thirty people without batting an eye.

**Reni** has speaking gifts too. She knows the difference between what's right and what's wrong, and she doesn't hesitate to help other people see that—even when it doesn't make her popular.

**Zooey** is another good spiritual speaker. She can always tell when someone is bummed out or ready to burst into tears, and she seems to know just the right thing to say to boost them up.

So obviously there is more than one kind of speaking gift, and you don't have to stand up at a podium and address a hundred people to use yours. Let's take a look at these gifts, one by one.

A *teacher* is a person who has a God-given ability to do three different things:

- Understand the lessons God teaches
- Explain those lessons to other people so they'll understand them too
- Help people see how they can use those lessons in their lives

Let's say you're in Sunday school and catch on right away to what the story of the Prodigal Son is really about. The other kids are saying, "How come the bad kid gets all the attention when the good kid always did was he was supposed to do?" and you speak up and help them see that the story's about how God will forgive us if we ask him to. Then you say, "I've been like the bad kid before. Anybody else?"

When you do that, you're using your *teaching gift*. You don't have to wait until you're out of college, ready to teach a whole class. You can do it now.

An *encourager* is a person who has the God-given knack for doing these two important things:

- See when people are discouraged or doubtful about God or wondering if *they* have gifts
- Say things that build those people up, reassuring them that they have gifts, and helping them remember that God loves them

Think about being on the playground at church. There's a little boy standing alone by the fence, kicking at the dirt. You go over to him and kick dirt with him.

Pretty soon you start talking, and you get him to tell you that the other kids made fun of him because he was afraid to go down the slide. You tell him you were scared of the slide when you were a kid, that it's okay to be afraid, and that you'll go down it with him if he wants. Pretty soon he's grinning from ear-to-ear and running for the playground equipment.

When you do that, you're using your *encourager gift*. You don't have to wait until you're a mom to do that. If you keep your eyes open, you can do it about every ten minutes!

A *perceiver* is a person who has the God-given talent to:

- Know what's true and what isn't, what comes from God and what doesn't
- Tell that, with confidence, to other people

Imagine that one of the kids in your Sunday school class is telling some of the other kids that he doesn't see what's wrong with playing with a Ouija board. After all, he says, it's just a game. You get a bad feeling about it. You know there's nothing in the Bible that says it's okay to mess around with stuff like that. You speak up and say, "That's a bad deal. We're supposed to get our answers from God, not some spooky thing like that." The other kids start nodding their heads.

You've used your *perceiver gift*. You don't have to wait until you've read the entire Bible to do that. Pay attention to what God is telling you now.

# HOW IS THIS A God Thing?

If God hadn't given his people speaking gifts, he would have to do all the talking himself—and not everybody is listening to him. He knows he can get our attention by putting his words into the mouths of the people he chooses. The Bible tells us about those people.

"We have different gifts, according to the grace given us," Paul wrote to the Romans. "If it is teaching, let him (you) teach; if it is encouraging, let him (you) encourage" (Romans 12:6–8).

But God wants those people who do the speaking thing to be *very* careful with their gift. James, one of the earliest Christians, wrote: "Not many of you should presume to be teachers ... because ... we who teach will be judged more strictly" (James 3:1). That's because a little bit of teaching—or speaking of any kind—can have a *big* influence on somebody, just the way a small rudder steers a big ship, or a little bit in the mouth controls a huge horse. Your tongue—that thing you teach with—is a small part of your body, but it does a big job.

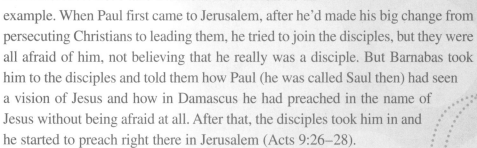

If you use your tongue wisely, you can make a real difference. Let's take Barnabas in the Bible as an example. When Paul first came to Jerusalem, after he'd made his big change from persecuting Christians to leading them, he tried to join the disciples, but they were all afraid of him, not believing that he really was a disciple. But Barnabas took him to the disciples and told them how Paul (he was called Saul then) had seen a vision of Jesus and how in Damascus he had preached in the name of Jesus without being afraid at all. After that, the disciples took him in and he started to preach right there in Jerusalem (Acts 9:26–28).

That wasn't the only time Barnabas used his speaking gift for the body of Christ. When the Greeks in Antioch decided they'd like to follow Jesus, Barnabas went there and encouraged them to stay with it, told them that God was with them, and even went to Tarsus and brought Paul back to teach them too. Basically, Barnabas just never stopped speaking up for God (Acts 11:22–26).

And Paul? He had every speaking gift in the book. One of the best examples is when he was in Paphos (on the island of Cyprus) and a sorcerer was putting down the message of Jesus. Paul looked straight at the sorcerer and told him he was a "child of the devil and an enemy of everything that is right" and *then* he caused the sorcerer to go blind. That definitely made believers out of the people who were watching (Acts 13:6–12).

You may not have the power to take away somebody's eyesight, but you do have the power to make a difference in people's lives—even if it's a little one—and every little bit counts.

#  CHECK Yourself OUT

Let's find out which speaking gifts God has given you. Take this little test, even if you didn't score high on speaking gifts on the quiz in chapter 1. You don't want to miss any of your God-gifts.

In each of the lists below, check the statements that are true for you and count up your checks for each list, putting the number in the space provided.

_____✓_____ I like to learn new facts.

_____ I like to study.

_____✓_____ I like finding out what new words mean.

_____✓_____ I always want to know the truth about everything.

_____✓_____ I'm a pretty good student.

✓ I don't have to be reminded to do my homework.

✓ I don't usually cry in front of people.

_✓_ I like to express my opinion.

_✓_ I think people will change their minds if they'll only listen to the truth.

_✓_ I can see how a story in the Bible can help me with a problem.

_8_ Total number of checks on List 1

LIST 2

_✓_ I like to make people feel better.

_✓_ I can tell how people feel about what I'm saying by watching their faces.

_✓_ I don't like to learn stuff I don't think I'm ever going to use (like dates in history).

_✓_ I like to do projects with other people.

_✓_ I learn things when I make a mistake.

_✓_ I stop helping people with their problems if they keep doing the same dumb thing over and over.

_✓_ I'm usually pretty cheerful.

_✓_ It's easy for me to make decisions.

_✓_ I finish what I start most of the time.

_✓_ I have a best friend I share my secrets with.

_9_ Total number of checks on List 2

List 3

_✓_ I can tell right away what's good and what's not.

_✓_ I can tell who's good to hang out with and who isn't.

_____ ✓ I say what's on my mind—it just kind of comes out of my mouth.

_____ ✓ I feel bad when other people mess up.

_____ ✓ I think it's good when somebody is sorry for what she's done.

_____ ✓ I always know when I've done something wrong.

_____ ✓ I pray for other people as much as I pray for myself.

_____ ✓ I get dramatic when I tell about something.

_____ ✓ I pay attention to what I'm feeling inside.

_____ ✓ I expect to be good.

_____ Total number of checks on List 3

**If you had seven or more checks in List 1,** you probably have the *gift of teaching.*

**If you had seven or more checks in List 2,** you probably have the *gift of encouraging.*

**If you had seven or more checks in List 3,** you are more than likely a *perceiver.*

If you have any of these gifts, God has plans for using you—but just in case that makes you a little nervous, read on.

## Girlz WANT TO KNOW

❀ *LILY: When I told my brother I had the gift of teaching, he said, "Figures. You always were a know-it-all." Is that true? Do I have to be a know-it-all to use my teaching gift?*

You definitely don't "have to." However, it's good for you to know that sometimes people with the gift of teaching do tend to have that problem, as well as some others. Teacher-types can be slow to accept other people's points of view. They may tend to feel smarter than other kids their age. It's easy for them to be sidetracked by a new interest and not finish what they've started.

But just knowing what those possible tricky areas are—and praying about them—and asking a friend to call you on them can keep you from being obnoxious about your teaching gift. The most important thing to remember is where the gift came from. When you give God the credit, you can't help but be humble.

✿   *ZOOEY: I'm excited about being an encourager, but it doesn't seem like other people always appreciate it. What's up with that?*

One of the problems encouragers sometimes have is that they're so anxious to help other people that they sometimes interrupt them before they even have a chance to express their feelings. Part of lifting people up is listening to them, letting them pour out what's hurting them before you tell them everything's all right.

Maybe we should call the speaking gifts "communicating gifts," because encouragement is a two-way thing. If you listen before you start talking, your help is more likely to be welcome.

✿   *RENI: I have that perceiver thing—but I'm not so sure it's a good thing. I say what I think, and then people tell me I'm trying to be the boss of them.*

Yeah, that can be a problem for perceivers. They feel so strongly about what's right and what's wrong—which *is* a good thing—that they tend to just blurt it out without thinking about how it's going to sound. You know, like if it's going to hurt somebody's feelings. Sometimes in their eagerness to point out what's *wrong,* they forget to mention what's *right.*

And when somebody else has a different opinion, you might want to look out! But you don't have to have those traits. You can work on *not* being blunt. You can remember to praise people for the things they do right. You can remind yourself to listen to what other people have to say. God will help you with all of that. Just ask and pay attention.

# Just Do It

Remember that a gift isn't a gift until you give it away. Whether you have a speaking gift or not, choose one or more of these activities to help you appreciate those gifts. You can turn any of these activities into something you and your "Gifts Group" can do together.

• Think of someone who has taught you something important about how to live a God-led life. Use your imagination to thank that person—whether it's drawing a picture, writing a letter, baking a batch of cookies, or just giving him or her a hug and saying, "Thanks!"

• Think of someone who has made you feel better when you were in a funk. Find your best way to tell that person what he or she has done for you—write a poem, pick some flowers, decorate a Scripture verse, or just say it with the best words you can find.

• Think of someone who has pointed out something to you that you were doing or saying that wasn't such a good thing on your part. Come up with a fun way to show your gratitude—draw before-and-after pictures of yourself, write a prayer, make your favorite craft, or just take the time to shake that person's hand and explain why you're doing it.

# Talking to God About It

Ready for your **TOY** prayer?

**Thank** God that there are people with speaking gifts—and give him some names of speakers who have touched your life.

Ask him to help **other** people you know to recognize their speaking gifts or to find someone to help them through the gifts of encouragement or teaching. Remember, God likes to hear names.

Ask God to help **you** develop your speaking gifts or to put people in your life who can encourage and teach you. Be sure to give God the specifics!

Don't forget that big-time *amen!*

If I had the courage, I would tell Janelle that . . .

She dosen't have to alwaqs wait for someone to ask her to play she can ank anyone.

# At Your Service

If anyone serves, he should do it with the strength
God provides, so that in all things
God may be praised through Jesus Christ.
*1 Peter 4:11*

**Suzy** has a serving gift. When the Sunday school class is doing a project, she waits until everybody's finished waving their hands around and giving ideas, and then she pitches in to cut and paste and paint. At home, she doesn't even think twice about fixing a snack for her mom when she's running late, or taking her sister's turn with the dishes so she can get to a youth group meeting.

**Kresha** does the serving thing too. Although she doesn't have much herself, she'll hand out parts of her lunch to everybody who forgot their money or their brown bags. She gets a big kick out of dumping all—and we do mean *all*—of her change in the collection plate at church, and she wouldn't hesitate to give something she just got for Christmas to a kid who got nothing.

**Zooey** serves by just *knowing* who has hurt feelings and how to cheer them up or at least make the pain not quite so frightening.

All three Girlz use their spiritual gifts to serve, but in completely different ways. Let's take a look at them.

A *server,* like Suzy, has the God-given ability to do two things:

- The hands-on stuff—practical things that need to be done if the church is going to keep on going.
- The things other people don't have time to do because they're so busy using *their* gifts.

Let's say your Sunday school class is putting together a presentation for next week's worship service. If you're a server, you might help glue the felt symbols onto the banner while some other kids write a skit. Then while they're practicing it, you'll probably help fix the juice and donuts for everybody—and find a cool way to arrange them on the plate.

A *compassion child,* like Zooey, uses her God-given gift of serving in a couple of different ways:

- Knowing how other people are feeling.
- Cheering up the sad ones and comforting the hurting ones with *actions.*

Imagine that you're at a Sunday school party and one of the kids gets mad because she doesn't win a prize in a game. She stomps off, lower lip sticking out, and everybody else whispers that she's a poor sport. But if you're a compassion child, you know something's not quite right about that. You sense that something else is going on with that girl, and you follow her over to the corner and talk to her. Pretty soon, she admits that her parents are fighting at home, and she's so worried about it that everything makes her mad. You give her a hug and invite her to be your partner in the next game. Pretty soon, she's smiling again.

A *giver*, like Kresha, serves God in two big ways:

- Giving money or anything else that's needed by the Christian community.
- Doing it with a big old grin on her face!

Think about your Sunday school class "adopting" a poor family at Christmas to provide them with gifts. Each kid in the class is supposed to bring in one toy for the family. If you're a giver, you do that and more, even if you have to make some sacrifices yourself. Maybe you don't have the money to buy a present, but you pick out two of your own toys and wrap them up. Perhaps you think about the mom of the family not being able to afford to bake Christmas goodies, so you whip up a batch of brownies with red and green sprinkles. You even come up with the idea of everybody in the class bringing in a Christmas ornament—and you make five really special ones yourself. You would even do more—but there just aren't enough hours in the day!

## HOW IS THIS A God Thing?

Peter—you remember, one of Jesus' original twelve disciples—wrote a letter to some Christians who were catching a lot of grief about their faith. In his letter,

Peter encouraged them to hang in there and trust God to help them—but he also told them to keep using their gifts, no matter how much people were picking on them. "If anyone serves," he said, "he should do it with the strength God provides, so that in all things God may be praised through Jesus Christ" (1 Peter 4:11). All through the New Testament, we see examples of people doing that.

- Stephen and six other guys were picked by the twelve apostles to make sure widows got the food they needed so the apostles could go on with their ministry, knowing the widows were being cared for (Acts 6:1–6).
- Epaphroditus (now *there's* a name for ya!) left his family and friends to travel with Paul and take care of his needs so Paul could focus on preaching and praying (Philippians 2:25–30).
- The jailer who was supposed to keep watch over Silas and Paul in prison washed their wounds, took them to his house, and even fed them (Acts 16:33–34).
- The churches in Macedonia were in extreme poverty, but they gave to Paul's ministry even more than they thought they could (2 Corinthians 8:1–7).
- The poor widow, Jesus pointed out, gave everything she had to the church (Mark 12:41–44).

None of those people did what they did because somebody made them do it or because they wanted to win some contest. They did it the way Paul said a real server does it: "not reluctantly ... for God loves a cheerful giver" (2 Corinthians 9:7).

By the way, there *is* a reward for using the serving gifts this way. God loves it—and he'll see that you have all the good things you deserve too (2 Corinthians 9:8).

# CHECK Yourself OUT

Let's find out which serving gifts God has given you. Even if you didn't score high on serving gifts on the quiz in chapter 1, take this little test anyway. You might be surprised.

In each of the lists below, check off the statements that are true for you and count up your checks for each list, putting the number in the space provided.

36

_____ I like it when other people say I helped them.

_____ I'm shy and get embarrassed real easily.

_____ I don't like to speak in front of the class.

_____ I like to do things the way I like to do them.

_____ I want everything I do to be perfect.

_____ I would rather be a follower than a leader.

_____ I like things like crafts, collections, and puzzles.

_____ I'm pretty neat in the way I take care of my stuff.

_____ If somebody asks me to help do something, I hardly ever say no.

_____ I would rather work on a short project than a long one.

_____ Total number of checks for List 1

_____ I like to make sure everybody feels good.

_____ I like to daydream.

_____ I make friends with people who don't have any friends.

_____ I ignore the bad things in people.

_____ I like everybody to get along with everybody else.

_____ It's easy for me to tell when somebody's not being honest.

_____ I feel happy when other people are happy.

_____ I don't like to be rushed in what I do.

_____ I like to play games that are quiet.

_____ I like to please everybody.

_____ Total number of checks for List 2

_____ I'm a happy person.

_____ I'm busy most of the time.

_____ I have a good imagination.

_____ I'm good at making and saving money.

_____ I like to give things without anybody knowing about it.

_____ I like to help when we have company at home.

_____ I don't get fooled very often.

_____ I'm loyal to my friends.

_____ I love to read.

_____ When I give a gift, I want it to be the best I can make or buy.

_____ Total number of checks for List 3

**If you had seven or more checks in List 1,** you probably have the *gift of serving.*

**If you had seven or more checks in List 2,** you probably have the *gift of compassion.*

**If you had seven or more checks in List 3,** you probably have the *gift of giving.*

If you have any of these gifts, God has plans for you. If that makes you a little nervous, read on.

# Girlz WANT TO KNOW

❀ *SUZY: Now I know why I like to help with stuff at home, especially when we have company or it's a special occasion—I'm a server. But you know what hurts my feelings? When people act like they don't even appreciate it! Is it wrong if I don't feel like doing things for them anymore?*

It isn't *bad.* In fact, it's a natural reaction. People really *should* at least say thank you. But when they don't, don't stop using your gift—getting people to say thank you isn't the reason for serving in the first place. If you keep in mind that you do special things for people because *God* wants you to and because he gave you the gift for being able to do those things, you won't be quite so disappointed when nobody makes a fuss.

However, since you're only human, try treating *yourself* after an evening or afternoon of waiting on people. Plan to take a glass of chocolate milk and some of those cookies you helped make into your room and curl up with a good book or a great CD. God will be happy to celebrate with you.

❀ *ZOOEY: I like to cheer people up because of my compassion gift—I guess. But sometimes after I've made somebody else feel better, I just want to go in my room and cry. My mom says I should stop listening to other people's problems if it upsets me, but then I wouldn't be using my gift, right?*

That's a tough one, Zooey. Your mom is just being a mom—she doesn't want you to ever be sad or upset. And she's right if it's hard for you to get happy again after an hour or so. Here's a good plan: when you've worked really hard to cheer someone up, spend some time doing something you like to do—baking a batch of brownies or swinging on the swing in the backyard or being with people who always make you laugh.

It's natural for a compassion child like you to take on the feelings of other people, but a steady diet of that isn't good for you. And if you're not healthy inside yourself, you definitely can't help someone else to be happy. Take care of *you* too.

❁ *KRESHA: How come some people are so stingy with their money and stuff? I'm about the poorest kid I know, and I give more than just about anybody else when we have canned food drives and that kind of thing. What's up with stingy people?*

You're like a lot of givers, Kresha. You have such a good time giving it all you've got, you just can't figure out why everybody doesn't go for it like you do. Be careful. Remember that there are a lot of different spiritual gifts and not everybody has the same ones.

Your friends may be working so hard teaching and serving and helping people solve their problems that they pretty much have to leave the giving to people like you. Before you decide they're *stingy*, thank God for your gift *and* theirs. When you're all doing your gift thing, you pretty much have it covered.

# Just Do It

Whether serving is your God thing or not, try one or more of these activities. This will help you appreciate that *somebody* has that gift. You can turn any of these into something you and your "Gifts Group" can do together.

• Think of someone who has done something for you so you could get something done that you needed to do. Use your imagination to come up with something you can do for that person—just because. Can you do her chores one day? Surprise him with a special snack for no special reason? Play with the younger kids so she can catch a nap?

- Think of someone who just knows what you're feeling, even before you say it. There's one thing you can know about that person, even if you're not officially a compassion child: that person would love a thank-you. Find the best way to do it—present him or her with a bunch of balloons, do the dishes without being asked, give an unexpected hug.
- Think of someone who has given something to you that you really needed. Give that person something he or she needs. Is it part of your allowance? A beloved stuffed animal for the night? Your second piece of pizza? (Uh, and don't forget to give cheerfully.)

# Talking to God About It

Ready for your **TOY** prayer?

**Thank** God that there are people with serving gifts—and give him some names of servers, givers, and compassionate people who have touched your life.

Ask him to help **others** you know recognize their serving gifts or find someone to help them through compassion or generosity. Remember, God likes to hear names.

Ask God to help **you** develop your serving gifts or to put people in your life who can help you where you need it. Be sure to give God the specifics!

And—as always—don't forget a good, loud *amen!*

My favorite daydream of saving the day is . . .

?I don't know?

# Make That a Combo

**Remember your leaders, who spoke the word of God to you.
Consider the outcome of their way of life and imitate their faith.**
*Hebrews 13:7*

**L**ily was the one who started the Girlz Only Club. She saw that there were other girls like her who needed a special bunch of friends to hang out and solve problems and learn stuff with—so she brought the Girlz together and got the whole thing up and running. Now that none of them can even remember what it was like *not* to have the Girlz group, Lily is still keeping it going—coming up with new ideas and figuring out ways to make them happen.

In the Girlz Only Club, **Reni** sees when the Girlz are getting off the track or a project is headed for disaster because it isn't organized. It doesn't bother her a bit to rein Lily in once in a while because sometimes Lily's enthusiasm keeps her from seeing the problems that might come up.

Both Reni and Lily have the ability to combine their *speaking* and *serving* gifts into another whole thing.

**Lily** has the spiritual gift of *leadership,* and she can use that in all of these ways:

- She has what we call "vision"—great ideas that are good for a group.
- She has the ability to "inspire" other people with her vision—get them excited about it so they take it on as their vision.
- She knows how to direct people in doing things to make that vision come true.

Let's say you're in a group in your Sunday school class, and together you're supposed to come up with an idea for a way to celebrate the Day of Pentecost in the class. Some people in the group are coming up with way-out stuff like setting off fireworks or hiring a flame-swallower, and other kids are giggling and carrying on, and nothing is getting done.

If you have the gift of *leadership,* you come up with an idea and take charge with it. You manage to get everybody quieted down and then suggest that the group get different people in the congregation who speak other languages to come in and say the Lord's Prayer in, like, French, Spanish, German, and Swahili. You explain that on the Day of Pentecost, everyone could understand what everyone else was saying even though they were speaking different languages.

Soon the other kids in the group pick up on your enthusiasm and start adding to the plan with some cool stuff of their own. You get somebody to write all the ideas down on a piece of paper, and then you ask for volunteers to do the different jobs. By the end of the class, your group has an amazing plan to show to the teacher, and the kids in the group say you should be in charge of doing it and they'll help. Get the idea?

**Reni,** on the other hand, has the gift of *administration,* which means:

- She understands how a group should be organized so it will work the best.
- She does the things that need to be done to get it organized.

Say, for instance, that your group starts making arrangements for that Pentecost celebration, and it isn't turning out quite the way everybody had hoped. If you have the gift of administration, you can see right away that it's because the leader is doing too much of the work herself and not letting anybody else do any of the fun stuff. You also figure out that one of the shy girls has a lot of drawing talent, but she's too bashful to speak up and volunteer to make a banner.

You use your administrative gift to get the group back together and ask the leader if the jobs can be divided up. And you suggest that the shy girl design a banner for some other kids to work on who aren't doing anything.

Without good leaders and administrators, the body of Christ would be going in about eighty different directions at once, and nothing would get done. It doesn't take a rocket scientist to figure out, though, that there won't be as many administrators and leaders as there will be servers and perceivers and teachers and all those other things.

If there were too *many* people with the combo gifts, the body—the church—would be in a mess. Who would do the work? So when it comes to leaders and administrators, it's just like putting on a play. Everybody wants to be the star, but not everybody has that gift. That's when the trouble can start. God, fortunately, has a way to keep it from getting out of hand.

# HOW IS THIS A God Thing?

There are a bunch of leaders and administrators in the Bible. Each one was chosen by God to lead a certain group of people or get a particular job done.

# Leaders

- God gave **Joseph** the tools he needed so that Pharaoh king of Egypt would put him in charge of his whole palace. (Stephen talks about it in Acts 7.)
- God gave **Moses** the power to mobilize the Israelites and get them out of Egypt where they were slaves. (Stephen talks about that in Acts 7 too.)
- God gave **Nehemiah** what it took to get God's people to work on rebuilding Jerusalem's wall, in spite of the people who were out there laughing at them and calling them names (Nehemiah 2:17–20).
- God gave **Joash** the idea for raising money to repair the broken-down temple in Jerusalem and the authority to get people to carry out his plan (2 Kings 12).

# Administrators

- **Joseph** wasn't just a good leader; he was a great administrator too. He figured out where all the good grain was and put a plan into action to store it for the coming famine (Genesis 41:46–55).
- **Aaron** was Moses' administrator, doing the things Moses couldn't quite do—like talk!
- **Eliashib** (aren't you glad names have changed since those days!) was the administrator for Nehemiah, organizing his fellow priests to rebuild the wall and dedicate it—no small task.
- Joash summoned **Jehoiada** (yikes!) to be his administrator for the Temple Rebuilding Fund-Raiser. Under his administration, enough money was brought in to buy all the building materials and meet the rest of the construction expenses too.

Yeah, there was some fussing and grumbling among the people who served under these leaders and administrators, but God never let that slide. As Paul explains it (in another one of those letters), they—and we—are supposed to *respect* those people in charge and *love* them, because they're working just as hard as we are (1 Thessalonians 5:12). It might look like a glamour gig, being the "boss," but it can be tough. Leaders and administrators have to:

- Keep watch over everybody (would *you* want that job?) (Hebrews 13:17).
- Take responsibility when somebody working for them messes up (Hebrews 13:17).
- Put up with jealousy and resentment from people who wish they had the job (Acts 7:9–10).
- Do and say things that aren't always popular with everybody (Acts 15:7–11).

God makes it pretty plain that we need leaders and administrators, and not everyone will be one. So, if you have the gifts of *leadership* and *administration*—God says take your job seriously and handle it with responsibility. And if your gift is to follow those leaders and administrators—God says look up to them and cooperate with them. After all, the body of Christ needs *all* of its parts, working together.

## ✓ CHECK Yourself OUT

It's time to check out whether you have the gifts of leadership or administration. Even if you didn't score high on "Gifts that Combine Speaking and Serving" on the quiz in chapter 1, take this little test anyway. You can never tell what you might find out.

In each of the lists below, check off the statements that are true for you and count up your checks for each list, putting the number in the space provided.

LIST 1

____✓____ People listen to me when I talk.

_✓_ My friends agree with me a lot of the time.

_✓_ My friends sometimes do things because I did them first.

_✓_ I get a lot of ideas that other people like.

_____ I like to be in charge.

_✗_ When I do projects with a group, they always turn out well.

_✓_ I make decisions pretty easily.

_✓_ I don't like to do the same things over and over.

_✓_ I'm not shy.

_✗_ I like big groups of people.

_7_ **Total number of checks for List 1**

_____ I like to make lists.

_____ I like to make plans.

_✓_ I get along with adults.

_✓_ I love to read about a lot of different things.

_____ My room isn't always that neat.

_✓_ I think it's important to follow the rules and obey the person in charge.

_✓_ I know when to change how I'm doing something so it will work better.

_✓_ I like to get done with the things I have to do pretty fast.

_✓_ I can tell right away how to do most jobs and projects.

_✓_ I like to do projects with other people.

_7_ **Total number of checks for List 2**

**If you had eight or more checks in List 1,** you probably have the gift of *leadership.*

**If you had eight or more checks in List 2,** you probably have the gift of *administration.*

Even if you had only a few checks in each list, you might be called on to be a leader or a leader's right-hand gal on some project someday. It would be a good idea, then, for you to read on and see what problems you might bump into along the way.

# Girlz WANT TO KNOW

✿   *LILY: I've always kind of been the leader in groups—I like that—but did you know you get criticized a lot when you're the leader? That I don't like.*

That's definitely one of the bummer things about being a leader. Everything you do is right out there for everybody to see, and there is always going to be somebody who sees it and doesn't like it. Maybe she says she wouldn't have done it that way or your way is dumb or she thinks you're being too bossy or not bossy enough—the list goes on and on!

When you get criticism when you're in charge, first look at what's being said and decide whether that person has a point or not. Then you can do one of three things:

1. If it looks like that person might be right, thank her for telling you and then do what you can to fix the situation.
2. If you can honestly say she's wrong, thank her for telling you anyway, and then do what you think is right.
3. If you can't decide, ask the group you're in charge of what they think. Be sure to tell them you want to know how they really feel, and not to be afraid of hurting your feelings.

Speaking of feelings, however, it's natural for yours to be hurt when someone criticizes your leadership, especially if you've been working really hard at it. It's okay to go off by yourself and have a good cry, vent to your mom, or spew it all out in your journal. But try not to:

1. Pout.
2. Say ugly things to or about the critic.
3. Talk to only certain people in your group about it and try to get them on your side.
4. Get mad and quit.
5. Hold a grudge after the whole thing is over.

· · · · · · · · · · · · · · · · · · · · · · · · · · · · · · · · · · · · · · · ·

❀  *RENI: It figures I'd be an administrator. Every time I get involved in something, especially at church, I end up being the one who writes everything down and turns everything in for my group. That takes a lot of time, and my parents get on me about being so busy doing it that I don't get my chores done at home. But isn't being an administrator more important than setting the table and putting my clothes away?*

The answer you probably want to hear is, "Yes, it's so much more important for you to be responsible to your church group than it is for you to do all those boring chores!" Uh, but that's not the answer. Your work at the church, as an administrator, is just *as* important as your home responsibilities, but

not more so. To live a God-
life, you have to have balance.
You need to be able to take
care of everything that's
expected of you so no one
thing slides all the time for
the sake of something else.
That isn't easy to do, especially in your case, but here
are some ways to make it
work:

1. Be sure you aren't taking on too many different church activities. It's better
   to do a good job at one than try to spread yourself out over four and have
   your parents on your back.
2. Get your chores done *before* you scoot off to do the church activities. It's
   easier to get that stuff done first than to try to do it when you're tired or
   rushed.
3. Ask your parents to help you schedule your time. Nobody expects you to
   be able to juggle everything on your own just yet. Maybe next year!

# Just Do It

You know the Bible verse at the beginning of this chapter? "Remember
your leaders, who spoke the word of God to you. Consider the outcome of their
way of life and imitate their faith" (Hebrews 13:7). Whether you think you're a
leader, an administrator, both, or neither, let's do a little "imitating" of the
people who have led you into good things. Remember that you can do this
activity with your "Gifts Group."

Think of someone who has been a good leader (this person might actually
be a good administrator, but sometimes it's hard to tell the difference, so we'll
just call them leaders this go-round). That person probably will be:

▣ Someone who has great ideas, but listens to yours too.

▣ Someone who gets you excited about doing something new.

▣ Someone who makes you feel like everything a group is doing is going to turn out great.

▣ Someone who makes you feel safe about his or her decisions for the group.

▣ Someone who keeps things interesting for you.

▣ Someone who is enjoyable for you to be around.

▣ Someone who makes being in a group a good experience for you.

Check the boxes above for those things that are true of this leader.
Who is that person? _Samantha Kamaka_

How are you now different because of this person's leadership? You can check off all of these statements that answer that question for you, and you can think of your own if you want to.

✓ I now know some thing(s) I didn't know before that person was my leader.

I've gotten to do things I wouldn't have done if my leader hadn't made it happen.

✓ I know I have a gift I didn't know about before my leader showed it to me and encouraged me to use it.

✓ I have friends I wouldn't have if that person hadn't brought the group together.

I'm not as afraid to do certain things as I was before that person was my leader.

Find a way to show how much you appreciate that person's leadership. Here are some suggestions—but, of course, you're free to use your gifts to come up with your own ideas. Whatever you do, be sure to include specific details that apply to your special leader:

- Make a giant thank-you card.
- Write your own words to a tune you know and "send" it in a singing telegram. (Either you sing it or have someone else do it—complete with balloons or candy, of course!)
- Make and present that person with a special award—a certificate, a ribbon, a medal, a mini-statue—something you've created yourself is the best.
- Write a letter to your pastor about the leader.
- If you have photos and other memorabilia from your group or project, make the leader a small scrapbook full of memories.

# Talking to God About It

It's time for the **TOY** prayer again. Here we go:

**Thank** God that there are people with leadership and administrative gifts—and give him some names of those people who have had an influence on your life.

Ask him to help **others** you know to recognize their combination gifts or to find good leaders to follow. God likes to hear you speak of them by name.

Ask God to help **you** develop your administration and/or leadership gifts or to put people in your life who can lead you or help you lead. Be sure to give God all the details.

(Pssst! Don't forget that major *amen!*)

I like to imagine myself leading a large group and performing this great ...

Music festivle.
It would have lots
of preerfomances of
dancing, singing and acting.

# The Trouble with Gifts

I am the vine; you are the branches.
If a man remains in me and I in him,
he will bear much fruit;
apart from me you can do nothing.
*John 15:5*

It was a bad day at Girlz Only Club. The Girlz had planned to make T-shirts for their team for the Sunday school picnic and field day. But things weren't going well.

**Lily** thought she had the best idea ever for the design to go on the front of the shirts, and she was pretty much bragging about it. **Reni** actually liked the design, but she hated it that she couldn't think of something as good, so she was picking Lily's idea apart. **Suzy** was over in the corner, just waiting for somebody to tell her what to do; she didn't offer any ideas because she figured as a *server* she wasn't as important as Lily and Reni. **Zooey** kept telling Reni to hush up because Lily always had the best ideas anyway. And **Kresha?** She thought of a way they could really make Lily's idea terrific, but she was afraid to speak up. The mood Lily was in, she was liable to snap her head off!

It's pretty obvious why the T-shirts weren't getting done. The Girlz weren't *using* their spiritual gifts—they were *abusing* them. Before you dash off to start putting your gifts to use, take a look at the pitfalls that are yawning open, waiting for you—and your gifts—to fall into.

# HOW IS THIS A God Thing?

Have you ever given a present to someone who totally loved it and used it all the time? Made you feel pretty good, huh? Like maybe you couldn't wait to give that person *another* present?

On the other hand, have you ever given a gift to someone who tore it up, was careless with it, or just stuck it away someplace and never used it at all? That probably made you feel plenty lousy, right? You probably don't feel like ever giving that person a present again.

God reacts to what we do with the gifts he gives us too. If you love the spiritual gifts God has given you and you take good care of them and use them constantly, God's going to like that. Chances are God will give you more and more ways to use those gifts, since you're getting so much out of them.

But if you sort of ignore your spiritual gifts, wish you had different ones, or use them to make yourself look and feel important—that doesn't set well with

God. You're going to miss out on a lot of neat opportunities because, basically, God isn't going to give them to you.

There are four main ways you can abuse your spiritual gifts. Check these out:

## 1. Feeling way too proud of your sweet self because you have a certain gift.

**Lily,** for instance, has the gift of leadership, and most of the time she uses it well. But in the example at the beginning of this chapter, she was flaunting it, bragging about her idea, and pretty much puffing herself up. God frowns on *pride*—when you think *you* are wonderful because of something *God* has done (like give you the gift in the first place and give you the chance to use it!). Here are a couple of examples:

- God threw Satan out of heaven because he was getting too uppity about his beauty and splendor (Ezekiel 28:12–19). (Although this verse refers to the "king of Tyre," many Bible scholars believe this passage also refers to Satan.)
- Naaman almost had to learn the hard way that he shouldn't think so much of himself that he couldn't accept word from a messenger, rather than from the great prophet himself (2 Kings 5:10–14).
- Jesus got in the faces of the teachers of the law and the Pharisees about taking the places of honor at banquets and the most important seats in the temple and how much they liked having people call them Rabbi (Matthew 23:5–7).

Just in case we miss the message of those examples, Peter makes it really clear for us in his first letter: "All of you, clothe yourselves with humility toward one another, because, 'God opposes the proud but gives grace to the humble.' Humble yourselves, therefore, under God's mighty hand, that he may lift you up in due time" (1 Peter 5: 5–6). So don't show off with your gift. Use it for one reason and one reason only—to make God happy that you're helping the body of Christ.

## 2. Being jealous of somebody else's gift.

**Reni,** in our opening example, hated it that everybody liked Lily's idea— even though she didn't have one of her own to share! Sometimes it just ate away at her that Lily did so many things well and so many people liked her. In fact, it ate away at her so much that it was chewing up Reni's ability to use her *own* gifts. Jealousy does nothing but destroy the person who feels it and the person who is affected by it, which is why God dislikes it so much. There are some major examples of jealous behavior in the Bible:

- Cain was so jealous of Abel, because God liked Abel's offering more than his own, that he killed his brother (Genesis 4:3–6, 8).
- Sarah was so jealous of Hagar (even though *she* was the one who arranged for Hagar to give Abraham a son!), and so mean to her, that Hagar ran away into the desert, where she could have starved (Genesis 16:6).
- Joseph's brothers were so jealous of him for being Jacob's favorite that they sold him into slavery (Genesis 37:4–28).
- Saul was so jealous of David, because people implied that David was a better warrior than he was (even though it was Saul himself who gave him the job!), he turned completely evil and plotted to kill David (1 Samuel 18 and 19).

Paul sums up what all these examples are trying to teach us. He wrote a letter to the people of Corinth telling them to stop their jealous quarrels about whom they should follow—Paul or Apollos. Paul said there was no room for jealousy because: "I [Paul] planted the seed, Apollos watered it, but God made it grow. So neither he who plants nor he who waters is anything, but only God, who makes things grow" (1 Corinthians 3:6–7). If we keep focusing on God, it isn't going to occur to us to be jealous of the other members of the body of Christ.

### 3. Thinking one gift is better to have than another one.

**Suzy and Zooey** both had the wrong idea about the gift thing. They were aware that they had gifts themselves, but Suzy thought her gift wasn't as important as, say, Lily's or Reni's, and Zooey thought Lily's gift was so important, Lily herself could do no wrong. God isn't crazy about either of those ways of thinking. The stories in the Bible tell the tale.

Paul used the body thing in his story. He said, "The eye cannot say to the hand, 'I don't need you!' And the head cannot say to the feet, 'I don't need you!' On the contrary, those parts of the body that seem to be weaker are indispensable [that means we can't live without them], and the parts that we think are less honorable we treat with special honor. And the parts that are unpresentable are treated with special modesty" (1 Corinthians 12:21–23).

Paul said, don't be dividing up the body parts! All the parts should have equal concern for each other. "If one part suffers, every part suffers with it; if one part is honored, every part rejoices with it" (1 Corinthians 12:26).

He also said it doesn't matter what gift you have, if you don't use it in love, you're abusing it. But if you use your gifts in love, every person is just as good as another. He used the giver as an example: "If I give all I possess to the poor and surrender my body to the flames, but have not love, I gain nothing" (1 Corinthians 13:3).

Yet there were still people who wanted certain gifts so badly, they were willing to *pay* for them! A sorcerer named Simon in Samaria saw that people were receiving the Holy Spirit when Peter and John placed their hands on them, so he offered them money and said, "Give me also this ability." Peter told him in no uncertain terms that his heart wasn't right before God and he had no part in their ministry. "May your money perish with you," Peter said to him, "because you thought you could buy the gift of God with money!" (Acts 8:18–23).

We call that kind of thinking *gift glorification*—making one gift seem more important than another, loving the gifts instead of the one who gave them. It's a lot like worshiping idols. That's why we need to keep these words of Paul's in mind:

"Whatever you do, work at it with all your heart, as working for the Lord, not for men, since you know that you will receive an inheritance from the Lord as a reward. It is the Lord Christ you are serving. Anyone who does wrong will be repaid for his wrong, and there is no favoritism" (Colossians 3:23–25).

## 4. Hiding your gifts and not using them at all!

**Kresha** didn't speak up—in the example at the beginning of the chapter—because just at that moment, she was kind of afraid of Lily, so she ended up not helping the group with her gift. Instead, she hid it. That happened to a guy in one of Jesus' stories too.

You've probably heard this story before. A man is going on a trip and he's leaving his property to his servants to take care of for him while he's gone. He gives one about $5,000, another about $2,000, and the third about $1,000. When he comes back, the man is pleased to see that the first servant has taken the $5,000 and doubled it (probably with good investments). He's also happy with the second servant, who has doubled the $2,000 he gave him to watch over.

But he isn't at all excited about the third servant, because he had the $1,000 buried the whole time for safekeeping, so all he has to give back is the same $1,000. The servant did that because the man yelled a lot, and he was afraid of him. He is even more afraid of him when the man yanks the $1,000 out of his hand and gives it to the servant who at this point has $10,000. Now that man has $11,000 (Matthew 25:14–30).

You probably understand what that story means, but look closely at one thing you might not have thought much about. The man doesn't give each servant the same amount of money. He gives them different gifts to take care of. It doesn't matter what gift God has given you; you have a responsibility to use it and make it grow for the body of Christ. It sure looks like the more you use it and the more good things you produce with it, the more God is going to give you.

Think of it this way: wouldn't you rather hear God say, "Well done, good and faithful servant!" (vs. 21) because you tried, than "You wicked, lazy servant!" (vs. 26) because you were too afraid to even let anybody see your gifts? Not a tough question to answer!

There are a number of different things that can tempt you to "bury" your gifts. People in the Bible faced them all:

- The **third servant**, as we've seen, was too *afraid,* and maybe *lazy* too.
- **Gideon** wanted *proof* that God could really use him (Judges 6:36–40).
- Paul exhorted **Timothy** not to let anyone look down on him because he was *too young* (1 Timothy 4:12).
- **Moses** didn't think he was as *qualified* as somebody else might be (Exodus 4:10–13).
- **The Invited Guests** in Jesus' parable were just *too busy* with other things (Luke 14:15–21).

Try not to let any of those things tempt you. Remember what Paul wrote in his second letter to those same people in Corinth: "Whoever sows sparingly will also reap sparingly, and whoever sows generously will also reap generously" (2 Corinthians 9:6).

## CHECK Yourself OUT

This can be a hard quiz to take because it asks you to look at some things in yourself you might not like so much. But that's okay. If you own up to your faults and weaknesses and ask God to help with those, you're just going to get better and better at using your gifts. So give yourself a hug for God and be as honest as you can. Put a *check* next to *every* statement that is true for you.

Sometimes in the past (maybe even once):

____ ✔ 1. I have wanted something somebody else had so much I did something about it.

____ ✔ 2. I have wished the nice things people were saying about someone else were being said about me instead.

_✓_ 3. I have hated it that someone else was getting more attention than I was.

_____ 4. I have told a lot of people about something I did that I thought was wonderful.

_____ 5. I have refused to admit I was wrong, even though I knew I was.

_____ 6. I have told a lie so I would seem better to people.

_✓_ 7. I have wished I could be in charge when I wasn't.

_✓_ 8. I have been glad I had something important to do when the other kids didn't.

_____ 9. I have thought somebody was perfect.

_✓_ 10. I have been afraid to say what my ideas were in a group.

_____ 11. I have skipped a church activity to do something I thought would be more fun.

_____ 12. I have refused to even try something new.

Keep in mind as you read the following that the results on this quiz are only here to help you know how you can be an even better gift-giver.

• **If you had any checks next to 1, 2, or 3,** be very careful about jealousy. Picture God at a party, giving you and each of the people you know a gift that is perfect for each individual person. Then remember that God gives out spiritual gifts that way too.

• **If you had any checks next to 4, 5, or 6,** keep an eye on your pride. Picture God giving you a present you've always wanted. Would you say thank you to yourself—or would you say thank you to God? If someone said, "Who gave you that?" would you say, "I gave it to myself!" or would you give the credit to God? Remember that it's the same with spiritual gifts.

• **If you had any checks next to 7, 8, or 9,** watch out for the urge to think of one spiritual gift as being better than another or any tendency to forget where the gift came from. Imagine opening presents from God in a group, with God watching, and saying to the kid next to you, "Hey—your gift is better than mine!" right in front of God, the giver. You wouldn't do that! So try not to do it with your spiritual gifts, either.

• **If you had any checks next to 10, 11, or 12,** make sure you don't bury your gifts instead of using them for God and God's people. Try to picture in your mind God giving you a gift, expecting you to open it in front of him so he can see the expression on your face, and you saying, "Thanks, God—I'm going to go dig a hole and bury this now." It's not gonna happen! Then don't let it happen to the spiritual gifts he's given you.

# Girlz WANT TO KNOW

It's all very easy to say, "I wouldn't do that!" or "That's not going to happen with *my* gifts!" But situations sometimes sneak up on us.

❁ *LILY: At school, they tell us we're supposed to "feel good about ourselves." So is it wrong to feel good that I have spiritual gifts in all the categories?*

God *wants* you to feel good that you're a teacher and a leader and a compassion child. He just wants the good feeling to come from him! He doesn't want you to feel good because you've made yourself all that you are—because you haven't. He doesn't want you to get a "big head" about all the things you can do—because without God you couldn't do them. And he doesn't want you to feel like you're better than other people because of your gifts—because you aren't.

Keep the good feelings focused on God and you'll be okay. How do you do that? Every chance you get, thank God for your gifts and give God the credit out loud to other people. Do that and you're just going to keep feeling better and better.

*ZOOEY: It's fine to say I believe that all the gifts are equal and act like my gifts are just as important as Lily's or Reni's. But when the programs come out, their names always come before mine. When people are handing out compliments, they always think of them first. Hardly anybody notices what I do. Is it wrong to want somebody to say, "Good job, Zooey?"*

We all like a pat on the back now and then, and God even tells us we're supposed to do that for each other. It's a bummer that the people you know aren't practicing that. But there are other things that tell you you're using your gifts the right way besides what people say.

Look for these "signs of applause" for your gifts:

- People are acting like they're enjoying what you've done, even if they don't say so.
- When for some reason you can't do your usual thing (you're sick or absent), people say, "Hey, where's the _____?"
- You feel important to the group, even if nobody actually says you are.
- You like doing things not many other people choose to do.
- Other people want to join in with what you're doing.
- Other people start to imitate the way you use your gifts.
- People come to you for help.

And, Zooey, knowing how you feel when nobody says, "Hey, good job," make sure you're doing that for others—including God.

*RENI: I know it's bad of me to be jealous of my best friend, but how do I stop the feeling? It's just there sometimes—I can't seem to help it.*

66

There are two things that might
help you:

- It isn't the feeling that's so bad
  as what you do with it. It's one
  thing to feel cranky because
  Lily is so amazing and at the
  moment you think you're not,
  so you wish she would trip and
  end up on the floor—and
  another to actually stick your
  foot out there so she'll fall over
  it! The action to take when the
  feeling starts creeping up is to
  pray—just as hard as you can.
- Good habits will eventually change bad
  feelings. Make it a habit to compliment
  Lily—and other people you may occasionally feel jealous of—on things about them you genuinely like. Make it a habit to say
  positive things about Lily to other people. Make a habit of being your own
  best self—with God's help, of course—so there's no time to be jealous or
  any reason to be.

# Just Do It

One of the very best ways to keep yourself from tumbling headfirst into the
pitfalls of *jealousy* and *pride* and *gift glorification* and *gift burying* is to help
each other avoid them. If you and your friends were walking together in a field
full of holes and sticker bushes and piles of yucky stuff, wouldn't you be saying things like, "Lily, look out!" and "Reni—behind you!" and "Suzy—yikes,
don't step in that!" You can do the same with holes and sticker bushes and piles
of yucky stuff that get in the way of our spiritual gifts. Here's how:

- Think of a friend who seems to be feeling like she's not good enough or who looks as if she's being left out of things or who is just in an angry or hurting place.
- By yourself or with your "Gifts Group" (this is a lot more fun with a bevy of girls!), dream up a way to honor your friend, to help her realize that she's special to God and has as much going for her (and the body of Christ!) as anybody else. Make it something just perfect for that girl. If she loves a parade, give her one, full of fun things that will make her laugh. If she loves a good book, make one for her, packed with love and delight that will bring a smile to her face. If she loves to eat, fix her a feast, a banquet of goodies that will show her how much she's loved.
- Make sure each person in your group has a part in making this "honor" happen—a part that makes the best use of each one's spiritual gifts. If you have a "giver," ask her to be in charge of coming up with the necessary funds. If you have a "server," ask her to be head of the food department. If you have an "administrator," let her get everybody organized.
- When you bestow this honor on your friend, make sure she knows that you are trying to point out her spiritual gifts to her. And be sure she comes out knowing God loves her even more than all of you do.

# Talking to God About It

**TOY** prayer time again!

**Thank** God for using this book to show you the possible pitfalls. Be specific about the ones you're particularly grateful to know about! (Like the ones you're most likely to jump into headfirst!)

Ask him to help **others** you know to climb out of the pitfalls they may have fallen into or to help them avoid the ones that are right in front of them. Remember—God likes to hear you speak of them by name.

Ask God to help **you** recognize your own dangerous areas—ones you've had trouble with in the past or the ones you're now aware could be a problem for you. Be sure to give God all the details. He likes it when you tell him everything.

Oh, and get the *amen* in there too.

The biggest pitfall for me is . . .

_____
_____
_____
_____
_____
_____
_____
_____
_____
_____
_____
_____

# Get It Together

**Now you are the body of Christ,
and each one of you is a part of it.**

*1 Corinthians 12:27*

If you've learned anything from the Girlz in this book, hopefully it's that your spiritual gifts are supposed to be used along with other people's spiritual gifts, all for the body of Christ—the community of Christian believers and the ones we hope will soon *be* believers. It isn't a solo act, an individual thing, or a chance to show off your uniqueness. It's all about getting it together for God.

For some people that just comes naturally. **Lily, Zooey,** and **Kresha** all love to get into a group of people and make things happen. They do their best work in teams.

But for other folks, it's a little harder. **Suzy** is a little bit shy, so she's always unsure of herself in a new group. **Reni** is independent, and a lot of times she'd rather just do something herself than have to put up with other people's whining, giggling, and carrying on.

Whichever general group you fall into—and we'll find out more about that soon—it's important for you to learn the right way to combine your gifts with those of other people so you can work like one body. Let's start with what God has to say about it.

## HOW IS THIS A God Thing?

In that letter to the Corinthians—which you're getting to know pretty well by now—Paul talked about the individual gifts they all had, but he reminded them over and over again: "You are the body of Christ, and each one of you is a part of it" (1 Corinthians 12:27). One big eye couldn't walk across the room, he told them, and one big foot couldn't see anything. Every part needed every other part, or the body—the church—just wouldn't work.

So what does it look like when every part—every person—is working together? Let's use an example from the Bible.

**Paul**—our letter writer and the man who turned from persecuting Christians to being persecuted himself because he was so committed to the work of Christ—had a pretty amazing combination of spiritual gifts. But even he couldn't spread the message of Jesus by himself. There were a number of different people who worked with him, but two of his most loyal coworkers were Silas and Timothy. The three of them made a great ministry team, each one doing his very different part.

**Silas** was chosen by the apostles and elders to travel to Antioch with Paul because he was a *leader* (Acts 15:22). When he got there, Silas also showed that he was an *encourager,* building up the Christian brothers, including Paul himself, in the work they were doing (Acts 15:32). Paul liked the way Silas's gifts wove together with his own. That's why he chose him for his ministry partner (Acts 15:40). It turned out that Silas also had *speaking gifts,* because he then preached, too, in the towns they visited with the message (2 Corinthians 1:19).

**Timothy** joined Paul and Silas and contributed his gifts to the effort. Paul showed Timothy that he had a *teaching gift* (1 Timothy 4:11–14), but Timothy also showed that he had a *servant's* heart, continuing to take care of Paul's work while he was in prison (Philippians 2:19–22).

**Paul** was pretty much the leader of the ministry, but he always gave Timothy and Silas credit for all the work they did. He even put their names on his letters, showing the people that the words of encouragement were coming from all three of them.

The women weren't left out of Paul's ministry team either.

**Priscilla** used her *hospitality gift* by taking Apollos, a promising preacher, into her home—where she and her husband Aquila also used their *speaking gifts* to explain the way of God to Apollos more clearly so he could work with Paul (Acts 18:24–26). She also opened up her home so a church could meet there (1 Corinthians 16:19).

The minute she became a Christian, **Lydia** started using her *hospitality gift,* insisting that Paul's group come to her house to stay (Acts 16:15). Later she took Paul and Silas in when they got out of prison, doing that hospitality thing again (Acts 16:40).

Then there was **Dorcas,** also known as Tabitha, who was definitely a *server* and a *giver.* She was "always doing good and helping the poor" (Acts 9:36). She was so loved for the way she used her gifts, Peter raised her from the dead! (Acts 9:40).

Those early Christians are models for us to imitate as we now make up the body of Christ like they did. Let's see where you are on that right now.

# ✓ CHECK Yourself OUT

There are two lists below. Decide which list *best* describes you, even if everything on the list isn't exactly like you. (It might help to check all the statements in both lists that are true for you and see which list has the most.) Remember to be completely honest with yourself.

_____ I am basically a loner with just a few friends.

_____ I like individual sports better than team sports.

_____ I would rather be around adults than kids my own age.

_____ I feel more comfortable around my parents than around my friends.

_____ I'd rather read a book than do almost anything else with my free time.

_____ I'm very independent.

_____ I have friends, but I enjoy being by myself too.

_____ I like to be first or best.

_____ I don't like opinions and views that are different from mine.

_____ I feel like I'm smarter than a lot of kids my age.

✓ I have quite a few friends.

✓ I like group games.

✓ I enjoy being around a lot of people at once.

_____ I really like working with other people on a project.

✓ I can sometimes be pushy when I'm working with people.

✓ I like being on a team.

✓ I don't often wish for some alone time.

✓ I have a hard time saying no when somebody asks me to help.

✓ I usually do more than I'm asked to do.

✓ I get along with parents, teachers, *and* friends.

**If List 1** sounds more like you, it might be harder for you to work as part of the Body of Christ than it is for some other people. That doesn't mean you're a loser and have to change your entire personality! It does mean that you'll probably be an important part of any group because you'll do a lot of things on your own to benefit everybody.

You might be the one to sit back and watch quietly while everybody is arguing over something, and then speak up and say the very thing that will solve the problem. You might be the one to encourage shy people to participate, while everyone else is so involved in the action they don't even notice who's being left out.

Just be sure you don't set yourself apart too much. You have things to contribute to the group, and the group has things it can teach you too. When you read the answers to the Girlz's letters in the next section, you'll see some ways to make being part of the group more comfortable for you.

**If List 2** sounds more like you, working with other "body parts" may be easier for you than it is for some people. That doesn't mean you should skip the rest of this chapter, though! You'll want to read the letters from the Girlz so you can avoid some of the traps that can trip up group-lovers—things like being domineering, getting so involved with the people you forget the project, and getting upset when other people in the group don't work as hard as you do. Besides, reading this chapter will show you how to help your fellow Christians who don't just pop happily into a group like you do.

# Girlz WANT TO KNOW

✿ *SUZY: I'm really shy, so even though I like the idea of working with other people on stuff, it takes me a long time to feel comfortable enough in a group to even raise my hand. By the time I feel like I belong, the project is over!*

In some ways, taking your time getting to know people can be to your advantage. That probably keeps you from jumping into things that might not be the best thing to get into in the first place. But you're right—it may be keeping you from having the best experience working with the "body" and giving all you can to it. Here are a couple of suggestions that might help you:

1. Look for long-term groups to get into instead of short-term ones. For example, work on getting to know the people in your Sunday school class, who are going to be together all year, instead of joining group projects that last only a few days or weeks. It's okay to do that because there are so many people who get bored with the same old group, there's a real need for people like you who would be content staying with the same group for years!

2. When you do have to take part in a short-term group project, go ahead and give yourself the first meeting to sit back and get your bearings. Find out who the leader is so you can go to that person one-on-one and say, "What do you want me to do?" Look for the person—or several people—you know you'll feel the most comfortable sitting next to and working closely with. Focus on the decisions that are being made so you can go home, think about them, and decide what you're going to say about them at the next meeting. Then, at that next meeting, sit near those comfortable people, remember those ideas you had at home, take a deep breath, and raise your hand. It'll be tough the first couple of times, but don't worry. Once you realize that nothing horrible is going to happen to you when you speak up (the ceiling isn't going to fall in—you aren't going to be laughed out of the room—that kind of thing), it will become easier and easier.

✿ *RENI: My problem working with other people is that sometimes they can be—so silly! Marcy McCleary giggles the entire time. Ashley Adamson does nothing but flirt with the boys. Shad Shifferdecker throws spitballs and makes stupid suggestions. It makes me want to scream, and sometimes I do, and then people say I'm pushy. But doesn't somebody have to take control?*

Don't you hate that? Most people who are slightly more mature than other kids their age do hate it when they get into a group where it seems like nobody else wants to work. The word to zone in on here is "seems." Chances are, not everybody in the group is actually enjoying fooling around and keeping the group from getting anything done. Some of them probably are wishing somebody would take control because they're getting pretty sick of it, but they can't be the one to do it because they don't know how or they don't have the confidence. You do. Since you feel this strong about it and you do end up "screaming" sometimes, you obviously have an *administration gift.* Next time you find yourself in a situation like that, try this:

Don't wait until you're ready to explode to say something. At the first sign of distraction—you know, when the first spitball flies—pipe up with something like, "Okay, guys—we have a job to do. Who wants to write down the ideas as we get them?" You won't feel like screaming yet, so you won't.

Focus on the people who respond to that—the ones who look grateful that you spoke up, the ones who volunteer to write things down, the ones who move physically closer to you. Ignore the people who are giggling, flirting, and hurling projectiles. If they don't get any attention for their antics, they'll stop.

Use your gift to get other people to give their ideas—even if they have to shout them over the noise at first. If you wait until there are other ideas written down, you won't appear to be bossy when you give yours.

Remember that it isn't all your responsibility. Where are the grown-ups when all this is going on? Don't hesitate to go to an adult and say, "This isn't working. We need a taller person in here!"

✿ *ZOOEY: I love to work in groups! The problem is, I get so interested in making friends with the other people, I forget what we're supposed to be doing. Then I get accused of "getting the group off the track." Am I doing that?*

You're an *encourager and a compassion child,* so naturally you're going to be more fascinated by the other people in the group than by the work. You probably are contributing a lot to the project because of that, and you aren't even aware of it. You're helping people feel good about themselves so they have the confidence to volunteer for things. You're cheering people up so they can forget about their problems and do something for the group. You're making that group a fun, safe place to be.

However, if people are saying you're getting the team "off the track," you might be doing your encouraging at the wrong time—like while the group is in the middle of making a decision. Maybe it goes something like this:

**LILY:** Does anybody have any ideas for the Mother's Day thing we're supposed to be planning for our Sunday school class? Suzy, how about you?

**SUZY:** No, I can't think of anything.

**ZOOEY:** Suzy, are you okay? You look like somebody hurt your feelings or something. Did they?

**LILY:** Um—yeah—Suzy, you do look kinda sad.

**SUZY:** I'm okay.

**LILY:** Anybody have any ideas? Kresha?

**ZOOEY:** Suzy, you know you can talk to us. We're your best friends!

**SUZY:** I'm okay.

**ZOOEY:** Are you sure? We can talk about anything.

**RENI:** Zooey! Give it up! We're trying to come up with ideas here—you're getting us off the track!

It isn't that the other Girlz are being cold. It's that you, Zooey, can forget everything else when somebody seems to need your attention. Why not change the conversation to something like this?

**LILY:** Does anybody have any ideas for the Mother's Day thing? Suzy?

**SUZY:** No, I can't think of anything.

**ZOOEY:** *(in a whisper to Suzy)* You want to talk later? You seem upset.

**SUZY** *nods.*

**ZOOEY:** Hey, Lil, what if we did something to show how we're growing up— you know, all bring in our baby pictures and put them next to pictures of us now?

See? You can do your job as *encourager* and *compassion child,* and still contribute to the whole group at the same time. It's all about the timing!

❀ *LILY: My mom says I do everything 150 percent. When I'm doing something by myself, it usually turns out to be a good thing. But when I'm in a group project—and I love group projects—I still do 150 percent and end up doing most of the work. Nobody else ever works as hard as I do, and I get so frustrated. Can you imagine how amazing our projects could be if everybody did their share?*

The thing is, your idea of what 150 percent is and somebody else's idea of what it is are not necessarily the same. That doesn't mean you're better than she is; it means the two of you are different. So, to avoid frustration in the future, try this:

1. Do your best because you love to go all out. Period. Full stop. Don't have expectations of other people based on what you expect of yourself. That isn't your job, no matter what gifts you have.

2. Make sure that your doing 150 percent isn't taking opportunities away from other people in the group. Maybe they aren't working as hard as you are because you're doing their share! Do the work you've been assigned and then ask if anyone needs help. That way you won't step on toes and take over.

3. Encourage other people in the work they're doing rather than just doing it yourself. Make sure when you "encourage" that you aren't making them think you could do a much better job than they're doing.

4. Keep reminding yourself—and ask God to remind you too—that the way the group works together and things the members learn along the way are just as important as the project itself. When you look back at a project, and you find yourself thinking, *That party we put together was awesome! But I miss working with those people. I wish we could do something together again,* that project made God happy. If you find yourself thinking, *The party turned out great, but, man, I'm glad it's over. Those people drove me nuts,* something went wrong. Ask God to help you with that one.

# Just Do It

Get your "Gifts Group" together. On separate pieces of paper, have each person draw and cut out the body part she thinks matches each of her gifts. For instance, if she's a giver, she might make a pair of hands. If she's a compassion child, she might make a heart. Each person should work separately on this part, not letting anybody else see what she's making.

When all the parts are ready, have each person write her name on each one.

Now find yourselves a big space on the floor or on a table, and try to put all the body parts together to form one big person. This probably will look pretty silly (and fun!), and there may be body parts missing—but you'll get an idea of how you all fit together to form the body of Christ.

If you want, tape your "body" to a larger piece of paper and keep it where you can all see it when you get together.

*And* if you want, check out what parts are missing. Do you need a "brain"? Are there any *teachers* in your group? Do you need eyes? Are there any *perceivers* around? Challenge yourselves to find people with those gifts and invite them into your "Gifts Group." This could be the start of an awesome team.

# Talking to God About It

This would be the perfect time to pray together with your "Gifts Group" or just with some friends who might also be interested in their gifts. (What? You haven't shown them this book yet?)

Gather in a way that's comfortable for everybody. You might form a circle and hold hands or touch knees. Maybe it'll be in somebody's quiet room or outside away from the noise of the house.

Then try this. Give each person a minute or two to think about the person sitting on her right and to find out what her gifts are. If she doesn't already know, it's okay to guess from the way she is every day. Then start with one person who thanks God, out loud, for the gifts of the person on her right, names the gifts, and maybe even points out how that person used them in the past. Go around the circle until God has been thanked for the gifts of every person in the circle.

If you want to—and you know each other very well and feel comfortable doing this—you can give each person a minute or two to talk to the person on her left and find out what she would like prayer for when it comes to her spiritual gifts. Does she need help finding out what her gifts are? Does she want to find a church family where she can share her gifts? Does she want her brother to stop making fun of her because she's into learning about her gifts? You can pray silently for that person on your left or you can go around the circle again.

However you pray your group prayer, don't forget the amen. You can get a *huge* one going with your fellow gift givers!

If I could form the perfect group at church, that dream group would include . . .

If you liked
The Uniquely Me Book,
you'll love its
fictional companion
Lily Rules!

# Lily Rules!

Nancy Rue

LILY
for
Class President

Zonderkidz

All right, guys," Ms. Ferringer said shrilly into the microphone. "Let's settle down now. You guys in the back—take your seats—we need to get started."

Lily Robbins looked around her and shook her head of wildly curly red hair. "Like anybody's listening to her," she said to her best friend, Reni Johnson, who was sitting next to her in the auditorium.

Reni pursed her lips, popping out her dimples. "She might as well be talking to a bunch of animals," she said.

"She is."

Lily pointed to the small group of seventh graders who had been arranging themselves into seats three rows down for the last ten minutes. Ashley Adamson was trying to place everybody boy-girl, amid much flipping of turned-up blonde hair and rolling of heavily shadowed blue eyes. Her cohort, Chelsea Gordon, was plucking at the boys' shirtsleeves and laughing up into their faces—practically drooling as far as Lily could tell.

"She's gotta be the worst flirt in the whole seventh grade," said Zooey Hoffman, who was sitting on the other side of Lily.

On the other side of Zooey, Suzy Wheeler shook her head, her shiny, straight black hair splashing against her cheeks. "Bernadette's worse."

Lily had to strain to hear Suzy, who was obviously trying to follow Ms. Ferringer's instructions even though none of the other students were.

"What Suzy say?"

That came from Kresha Ragina, who was sitting on the other side of Reni, squinting from behind her wispy, sand-colored bangs.

*This has got to be hard for Kresha,* Lily thought.

Kresha was from Croatia, and although her English was improving all the time, she still had trouble sorting out words when there was chaos.

"She said Bernadette is the biggest flirt in the seventh grade," Reni told her.

"What is 'flirt'?"

Lily let Reni explain it to Kresha while she studied Bernadette. She was definitely tossing her head of shoulder-length, curling-ironed hair at Benjamin. But she had some pretty stiff competition from Chelsea and Ashley and about five other girls who were all snatching ball caps from the heads of boys who, they obviously knew, would go to great lengths to get them back.

*What is so fun about being around a bunch of absurd little creeps?* Lily thought. *Give me my Girlz anytime.*

She looked down the row on either side of her at Suzy, Zooey, Reni, and Kresha — the Girlz Only Club — and gave a contented sigh. Just then the microphone squawked with feedback up on the stage, which sent everybody into a frenzy of moaning and ear covering. Ms. Ferringer took that opportunity to shout, "Quiet down now, guys, or we won't get any class officers elected today."

At that, Ashley half-rose in her seat and made a loud shushing noise. The auditorium got as quiet as it was probably going to get.

"She *so* thinks she runs this school," Zooey whispered to Lily, round eyes rolling.

Lily rolled hers back and then settled into the seat. This was going to be a long assembly, watching the popular kids get elected to office. It was going to give them still another reason to act like they owned Cedar Hills Middle School.

"We're three months into the school year," Ms. Ferringer said into the mike.

"Ya think?" somebody in Ashley's row shouted.

A bunch of kids laughed. Lily didn't.

"And now that you've all had a chance to get to know people who've come here from other elementary schools, you get to elect officers."

"She talks like one of the kids," Reni whispered to Lily. "No wonder she doesn't have any control."

Lily nodded. Even now in the row in front of them, Daniel and Leo were launching folded-up pieces of paper from rubber bands.

"Here's how this is going to work, guys," Ms. Ferringer was shouting, even though she was practically swallowing the microphone at this point. "Quiet down, now—I will take nominations for president first."

Hands went up in Ashley's row, and somebody yelled out "Benjamin!" The rest of them clapped like the voting had already happened.

"If you nominate someone," Ms. Ferringer went on, "you have to give a nominating speech—not longer than a minute—about why you think your candidate would make a good officer."

Bernadette waved her hand more wildly than ever. Ms. Ferringer pointed to her, and Bernadette bounced out of her seat and up the aisle toward the stage, hair swinging down her back in perfect curls.

"I want to nominate Benjamin!" Bernadette squealed into the mike. Ashley's row erupted.

Ms. Ferringer paused, dry-erase marker in her hand. "What is Benjamin's last name?" she asked.

Bernadette looked at her as if she'd lost her mind. "Hel-lo-o," she said. "Weeks!"

"Like everybody in the world knows him," Reni muttered to Lily.

While Ms. Ferringer wrote Benjamin's name on the white board, Bernadette dazzled the auditorium with a smile and said, "I nominate Benjamin because—he's so cute!" Then she squealed again and tossed her hair. "No—just kidding—I mean, he *is* cute—but that's not why he should be president. He should be president because—like—who else knows as many people as he does?"

Ashley's row cheered as if Bernadette had just delivered the Gettysburg Address, and Bernadette bounced back to her seat.

"Any other nominations?" Ms. Ferringer said.

To Lily's surprise, Ashley raised her hand.

"Who's she gonna nominate?" Reni whispered to Lily. "I thought her whole crowd would be voting for Benjamin."

"Come on up," Ms. Ferringer said to Ashley. Although the auditorium was still one big squirming mass, she looked pleased, as if things were going rather well. Lily looked at the clock. They still had fifty endless minutes to go.

When Ashley got to the microphone, she took a few seconds to connect with her group, who all whistled and cheered before she even said anything. Then she leaned into the mike, gave a somewhat evil smile, and said, "I nominate Lily Robbins."

Lily immediately knew she was starting to blotch up like she always did when she wanted to crawl into a hole and die. Ashley would do *anything* to humiliate Lily.

"I think Lily Robbins should be president," Ashley was saying, still with that sarcastic smile on her face, "because she's, like, way responsible, and she's totally serious about everything." She paused, as if she were expecting boos. There were a few exaggerated snores and one shout of, "Oh—so she's a geek!" But it apparently wasn't enough for Ashley, because she added, "And she's teacher's pet in, like, every class."

That did it. The auditorium exploded with put-down laughter and cut-down comments. Lily felt like she was being sliced and diced for a trip to the frying pan.

"So if you like that kind of a person," Ashley shrieked over the commotion, "vote for Lily Snobbins—oh, sorry—Robbins."

"I'm gonna throw up," Lily said to Reni.

"Are you really?" Zooey said. "Do you want me to go to the restroom with you?"

"No!" Reni said. "You have to stay here and vote!"

"Like it's gonna matter," Lily said as she watched Ashley wiggle triumphantly back to her seat. "Nobody's gonna vote for me after that speech."

"Will the two candidates please hide your eyes?" Ms. Ferringer said from the stage. "We will vote by raising hands. Teachers—are you ready to count?"

Several of the teachers and administrators stood up, including Officer Horn, the school's policewoman, who was known among the students as Deputy Dog. Right now she was living up to her nickname as she came down the aisle and stood like a rottweiler at the end of Ashley's row.

"She's gonna make sure nobody raises more than one hand," Reni said. "Cover your eyes, Lily."

Lily did, gladly. There was no way she wanted to see how badly she was about to be defeated.

"All those for Benjamin raise your hands, please," Ms. Ferringer said.

Lily could feel arms waving in front of her and behind her. She could also hear Ashley's friends giving a victory whoop.

"All those for Lily—"

There was a lot of rustling around—more than Lily expected—and beside her, she heard Reni gasp.

"Lily!" she whispered. "I think you just won!"

Lily shook her head. "No way!" she whispered back.

There was a long, unbearable pause, and then Ms. Ferringer cried out, "Lily Robbins is our seventh-grade class president!"

She sounded as amazed as Lily felt. Lily pulled her hands away from her eyes and looked around, stunned. The first person she saw was Ashley, popping up out of her seat.

"That's not right!" she shouted. "We demand a—" She turned abruptly to her friends. "What's that thing called?" she said.

"A recount!" Benjamin called out.

Ms. Ferringer hesitated, as if she were considering it. Down in the front, Mrs. Reinhold—the English teacher—was shaking her head firmly. Ms. Ferringer glanced down at her and shook her head at Ashley.

"She's as scared of Mrs. Reinhold as we are!" Suzy said.

At least, that was what Lily *thought* Suzy said. She was still so flabbergasted, she wasn't sure of anything she was hearing.

But Ms. Ferringer erased Benjamin's name from the board and opened the nominations for vice president. Bernadette was, of course, on her feet at once, but Lily missed most of what went on for the next few minutes.

*I'm president!* was all she could think. *I'm president of the whole seventh-grade class!*

Visions of standing before them all, gavel in hand, filled Lily's head. She'd have to rethink her wardrobe, of course. You couldn't conduct class meetings in jeans. She'd definitely have to tame her hair—and probably get a more conservative binder since hers had Winnie the Pooh on the front. Then there were going to be bills and amendments to introduce and all that stuff that she wasn't quite sure about yet, but if she got some books to read about government and maybe interviewed the mayor—

She was imagining herself putting some important-looking document on the principal's desk when Reni nudged her and said, "Raise your hand!"

"Why?" Lily said, as Reni grabbed her wrist and jerked her arm into the air.

"You're voting for Ian Collins!"

"Who's Ian Collins?"

"I don't know—but he's not Benjamin!"

Lily looked with glazed eyes at the dry-erase board. The names Ian Collins and Benjamin Weeks had been written there, and votes were obviously being taken. It looked as if Benjamin's name was about to be erased again.

"Ian Collins is our winner!" Ms. Ferringer said—although she looked once more at Mrs. Reinhold for the final nod. Ashley's group stood up and chanted, "Recount!"

Lily ignored them and checked out Ian Collins, who was sitting across the aisle, being congratulated by his friends.

*Oh, yeah,* Lily thought. *I know him.* He was in a couple of her classes, but she'd never noticed him much, probably because he wasn't obnoxious. Most of her attention to boys had been attracted by the stupid things they always seemed to be doing.

Lily looked curiously at Ian. He was taller than a lot of the boys in seventh grade, most of whom still came up to about Lily's shoulder. He was skinny, and he wore his almost-blond hair short but not weirdly shaved anywhere, and he was currently grinning at a couple of his buddies, brown eyes shining from behind a pair of wire-rim glasses.

*Yikes,* Lily thought, *we elected somebody who wears glasses?*

That made her a little nervous, actually. If he wore glasses and he was still popular enough to get voted in, he must be pretty cool. Cool was never a word other kids used to describe Lily. She knew that. Working with Ian could be humiliating.

But Lily straightened her shoulders. *I'm president now,* she told herself. *It's all about confidence.*

Just then, Ian looked across the aisle and caught her eye. She gave him a quick wave. He grinned, and it wasn't an "oh, brother, I have to work with a dork" smile but one that said, "All right."

It was enough to inspire Lily to shoot her hand up when Ms. Ferringer said, "Nominations for secretary?"

"Suzy Wheeler," Lily said when Ms. Ferringer called on her. She could hear shy Suzy protesting as Lily rose to give her nominating speech, but Lily ignored her. Suzy was the neatest, most organized person on the planet, which was what Lily told her audience. When she was finished, Ashley's whole row stood up like one person and shouted, "Boo!"

Before Lily could even start to turn blotchy, Deputy Dog was on them, hauling the whole crowd of them out of their seats and up the aisle. When the vote was taken, there was barely anybody there to vote for their candidate, Chelsea. Suzy was elected by a landslide.

From there it was a piece of cake getting Ian's friend Lee Ohara elected treasurer and Zooey elected historian. Kresha gave an adorable speech about Zooey's experience with scrapbooking. Lily was convinced most people voted for Zooey because they thought Kresha's accent was cute. By the time the assembly was over, none of Ashley's crowd had been elected to office, and three of the five Girlz had.

It was the two who hadn't — Kresha and Reni — who made Lily play down her victory as they all headed off for their second-period classes. Reni and Kresha seemed happy for them, but it struck Lily that this was one of the few times they wouldn't all be doing something together.

Lily changed the subject to what they were all going to do at their Girlz Only Club meeting at Zooey's after school. She was sure that made Kresha's smile a little wider and Reni's dimples a little deeper.

By the time she got home that day, however, Lily was about to pop to really share the news in style with somebody. Mom and Dad, she knew, were going to be so proud. And besides, with her older brother Art always winning at band contests and her little brother Joe hauling home trophies for every sport in life, it was nice to be a winner herself for a change.

She was a little disappointed when she first got home that Dad wasn't available. The Robbins family was adding on to the house — in preparation for a new kid they were hoping to adopt — and Dad was tied up in his study with a tattooed construction worker, poring over blueprints.

Mom didn't get home until almost 5:30, and by then Lily was ready to explode. She met Mom at the door from the garage, and said, "Guess what!"

"You got through the entire afternoon without getting into a fight with either of your brothers," Mom said. Her mouth twitched the way it did when she was teasing.

"No!" Lily said. "I mean — I did — but that's not my news."

"That's enough news for me," Mom said. "I may go into shock." She put two bags of groceries on the kitchen counter. "Help me get the rest of the stuff out of the car, would you, Lil?"

"Mom — wait — you hafta hear my real news!" Lily grabbed both of her mother's hands. "I was elected class president today!"

Mom gave the expected jolt of surprise, her brown-like-a-deer's eyes widening.

But then she pointed to one of the kitchen chairs and said, "Sit down, Lil. I think we need to talk about this."

## Chapter 2

Lily felt herself deflating, kind of like a bicycle tire with a slow leak. "Aren't you happy for me, Mom?" she said.

"Of course, I am," Mom said. There was a "but" coming, though. Lily could tell by the way Mom tightened her ponytail and then folded her hands on the tabletop.

"I just want you to think about this," Mom said. "You already have Girlz Only, plus you're going to want to be in the Shakespeare Club production again in the spring."

"But—"

"*And* you're still recuperating from pneumonia—and we have the adoption coming up—"

"But—"

"*Plus* you need time for studying and church activities." Mom gave Lily another long look. "I just don't want you spreading yourself too thin. You know how you go after things 200 percent."

"But I can do it all, Mom!" Lily said. "And this is, like, the most important thing that ever happened to me in my whole life!"

A voice from the doorway said, "Dude, did you win the lottery or something?"

Lily barely glanced at her sixteen-year-old brother Art who stuck his reddish-brown head in the refrigerator.

"I'm class president!" Lily said.

"On top of everything else she has going," Mom said.

Art pulled his head out, a container of salsa in his hand. "Don't worry about it, Mom," he said as he began to forage in a cabinet. "All the class president does in middle school is get her picture in the yearbook. By tomorrow everybody'll forget who it is."

"Okay, look," Mom said to Lily. "You and your father and I will sit down and talk about this and make sure this is something you should be taking on."

"Can we do it as soon as that construction guy leaves?" Lily said.

"No—I have dinner to get on the table." Mom pulled a bag of tortilla chips out of Art's hand. "That means no snacks."

"Tonight, then?" Lily said. She knew her voice was pleading—bordering on whining, even—but this was *way* important.

"Dad and I have a meeting at the adoption agency tonight," Mom said. "Now don't go ballistic on me—we'll get to it." She stood up. "You two go get the rest of the groceries out of the car."

Lily could feel her face blotching as she followed Art out the door.

"Don't start freaking out," Art said as they headed through the garage. "Like I said, it's not that big of a deal. You don't even do anything."

"Huh," Lily said.

Maybe class president used to be a job where you didn't do anything, but it wasn't going to be that way this year, not with her in office. This year, she was going to shake the whole place up—*if* Mom and Dad would let her.

After they left for their meeting that night, Lily holed up in her room with her talking-to-God journal and her dog Otto. He busied himself chewing on an old toothbrush he'd pulled out of the trashcan while Lily poured out her dilemma to God.

*I think it was a miracle that I got elected,* she wrote, *which means you meant for it to be. Please work on Mom and Dad so they'll see that. And please let me get along with that Ian kid, even though he's a boy. And please don't let Kresha and Reni feel left out. And please make me the best president of the seventh grade that ever was.*

Lily paused to consider that last request. From what Art had said, it wasn't going to be that hard to surpass everybody else who had ever held the office.

*But I'm still going to be amazing, God,* she wrote. *I just have to be positive.*

The next morning when Lily got to school, she headed straight for the bench by the stairs where she and the Girlz usually met before classes. She knew they'd be sympathetic.

No one else was there yet, and Lily had just pulled off her backpack when Deputy Dog strolled up, giving Lily a big, square grin.

"Congratulations, Robbins," she said, sticking out a hand for Lily to shake.

She pumped Lily's arm enthusiastically, but Lily barely noticed. Her mind was already forming the outline of an idea.

"I really want to make a difference while I'm in office," Lily said to her. "Maybe you could help me."

Deputy Dog folded her arms. "How so?" she said.

"Maybe we could get some rules changed that aren't really that fair."

Deputy Dog grunted, but she didn't hook her thumbs into her belt, which would have been the sign that she was getting mad.

"There are a few I'd like to see changed myself," Officer Horn said, "but most of them aren't made by the administrators here — they're set up by the county school board. We're talking about the big boys."

"Huh," Lily said.

Deputy Dog narrowed her eyes. "I know that look, Robbins."

"What look?" Lily said. She tried to get any look at all off of her face.

"That nobody's-going-to-stop-me look." Deputy Dog leaned closer to Lily. "You're a good kid. Don't go getting yourself in trouble, y'hear me?"

"There won't be any trouble," Lily said. "I'm going to do everything right."

Deputy Dog gave another soft grunt. "Maybe you better check with me before you do anything serious," she said. "I know Ms. Ferringer is your class advisor, but — "

She didn't finish the sentence. She didn't have to. Lily knew what she meant. Poor Ms. Ferringer had looked like she was going to collapse after yesterday's assembly.

Zooey, Suzy, and Kresha arrived then, and Deputy Dog sauntered away.

"What were you guys talking about?" Zooey asked.

Suzy knitted her delicate black eyebrows together. "Are you in trouble?"

Lily gave a nonchalant shrug. "We were just talking about class president stuff," she said. She stole a glance at Kresha. She was sure she saw something lonely flicker through her eyes. It was a bummer Reni didn't meet with them in the mornings, or Kresha would have had somebody who knew how she felt. But Reni practiced her violin in the orchestra room every day before school.

Just then, Lily saw Reni hurrying by, violin case in hand. Walking with her was a girl Lily had seen only a couple of times.

"Reni! Hi!" Kresha shouted.

Reni turned from her conversation with the other girl and smiled vaguely in their direction. Without stopping, she hurried on toward the music wing.

"Well, excuse me!" Zooey said.

"She not wave," Kresha said, forehead wrinkled.

"She was in a hurry," Suzy said. "She's late for practice."

*Huh*, Lily thought. *Reni's my best friend. What was she doing with that other girl?*

"That's Monique Masterson," Zooey said. "She's in the dumb classes with me."

While the other Girlz jumped on Zooey for calling herself dumb, Lily pushed the jealous pang out of her chest. She and Reni had been best friends forever, and they always would be. No need to worry.

In fourth period that day, Ms. Ferringer was supposed to give a geography test. When they arrived for class, however, she looked more nervous than any of the students. She was pulling everything out of her desk drawers and muttering to herself.

"What's with her?" Chelsea said, curling her lip.

"Who cares?" Ashley said.

But Marcie McCleary was happy to inform them. "She can't find her keys."

Lily tried not to look suspiciously at Marcie. The way she dressed these days, chains hanging from her jeans and fake tattoos dotting her arms, it made her a prime suspect when anything was missing. Marcie had teamed up with a bunch of gang wannabes at the beginning of the year and was always being called to the office for one thing or another.

Ms. Ferringer didn't bother to question Marcie or anybody else. When the bell rang she gave the bottom drawer of her desk one last inspection and then stood up and began frantically passing out test papers.

"Get out a pen or pencil," she said. The way her eyes were darting all around, Lily was sure she wouldn't have cared if they'd written in crayon.

"She's freaking," Reni whispered to Lily.

"What's so important about a bunch of keys?" Lily whispered back.

As soon as Ms. Ferringer had passed out the papers, she dove back to the desk and continued her search. Within seconds, she looked as if she'd forgotten there was even a class in the room.

Lily finished the test quickly, and even after she checked over all her answers twice, most of the other kids were still working. She noticed that on the other side of the room, Ian Collins had put his pencil down and was staring into space.

*At least I have a smart vice president,* Lily thought. She also thought about the note she'd gotten in first period from Ms. Ferringer, saying they would have an officers' meeting during lunch. Lily wished she could jot down some ideas, but that would mean getting stuff out of her backpack, and Ms. Ferringer wouldn't let them do that during a test. She at least tried to be strict about cheating.

So Lily leaned back in her seat and looked around to see if everybody was almost done. Reni was, and Suzy. Also Lee Ohara. Ashley, however, was still hard at it — pencil scratching across her paper. As Lily watched her, she stopped writing and slid her paper ever so slightly toward the edge of her desk.

*It's gonna fall on the floor,* Lily thought.

And then it did. Ashley didn't reach down to scoop it up, because Benjamin was too quick for her. He leaned down, grabbed the paper, held it up so he could brush the dirt off of it, and then slowly handed it to her.

Ashley gave him a sly smile as she took it back from him

19

*Oh, brother,* Lily thought. *She* so *did that on purpose!* She shook her head. There they were, in the middle of a test, and Ashley was flirting, right under Ms. Ferringer's nose.

Currently, Ms. Ferringer's nose was in the closet, where she was tossing stuff behind her, still muttering to herself. Ashley probably could have stood up and hugged Benjamin and Ms. Ferringer would have kept on looking for her keys.

Lily slid down in her desk and was about to go back to daydreaming about the upcoming officers' meeting when she saw Chelsea's paper fall off of *her* desk. Benjamin went after it and did the same routine as he'd done with Ashley's paper.

*Best friends competing for the same boy,* Lily thought. *What is the deal?*

Chelsea, it seemed, was willing to go a step further than Ashley. She leaned across the aisle and whispered something to Benjamin. Lily looked nervously at Ms. Ferringer, who was now on her hands and knees, peering around on the floor. She started to bring her head up, but she banged it on the underside of her desk.

"Who's talking?" Ms. Ferringer said. "You are taking a test!"

"Ya think?" Ashley murmured. But she and Chelsea and Benjamin and Bernadette locked their eyes on their papers, pictures of innocence, all of them. By the time Ms. Ferringer got to her feet, they were dotting their final i's.

"Time's up," Ms. Ferringer said. "Turn in your papers."

As tests made their way to the front, Lily couldn't help looking at Ashley and her friends again. They were wearing smiles so smug that they might as well have had "WE JUST TALKED DURING A TEST AND GOT AWAY WITH IT!" written across their foreheads.

Ms. Ferringer missed it. She was busy writing something on the board. THE SEMESTER PROJECT, it said.

"I hate doing those," Ashley said. "They're so lame."

"No problem," Benjamin said. He looked at Ashley and winked at her. She melted. *Ashley's now ahead by one flirt,* Lily thought.

"This is to be a full-length report on a country that you will draw out of a hat," Ms. Ferringer was saying. "Tomorrow I will give you an outline of what I want in it."

"If she can find it," Benjamin whispered.

Ashley and Chelsea laughed, and Ms. Ferringer looked at them blankly. Lily was starting to feel sorry for her.

"You'll have to include maps and sketches," Ms. Ferringer went on. "Don't wait until the last minute, because this is going to be worth half your grade."

Lily waited for Ashley and Benjamin and Bernadette and Chelsea — the ABCs — to protest. The girls looked at Benjamin, who winked at each of them this time. Then they all got that superior expression on their faces that made Lily squirm.

But Lily forgot about the four of them when the bell rang and everybody left for lunch except her and Suzy and Ian and Lee. Zooey hurried in a few minutes later, as Ms. Ferringer was instructing them to put their chairs in a circle. Lily could tell she was still thinking mostly about her keys, though, which was fine, because Lily was prepared to run the meeting anyway. She'd even covered her Winnie the Pooh binder with plain white paper the night before.

When they were all settled, Lily said, "The meeting will now come to order." She'd seen that on TV one time, and it seemed like an important thing to do. Of course, in this case, nobody was out of order to begin with, but Lily said to Suzy, "Write down everything that happens."

Suzy pulled a perfectly sharpened pencil out of the zipper pouch in her binder and went to work.

"I think the first order of business," Lily said — another thing she'd heard on TV — "should be to decide when we're going to meet.

I think it should be once a week, only not after school because I have another meeting every day after school."

"I move we make it on Wednesdays," Ian said.

"You 'move'?" Zooey said. "What's that mean?"

Lily hoped Ian knew, because she didn't.

"It means I'm making a motion," Ian said.

"Oh," Zooey said. She blinked a couple of times.

"He's suggesting something," Ms. Ferringer told her. "Although I'm not sure we have to be that formal."

"I do," Lily said. "It'll keep us organized." Then she made a mental note to look up things like motions the first chance she got.

"You should ask if there's a second to my motion," Ian murmured to Lily.

"Oh, yeah," Lily said. "Is there a second to Ian's movement?"

"Motion," Ian whispered.

"I second it," Lee said.

*Yikes,* Lily thought. *I have a lot to learn!*

"Now you ask for all those in favor to say 'aye,'" Ian muttered to Lily.

"All those in favor say 'aye,'" Lily said.

Everybody said "aye," though Zooey was still looking confused.

"Your first motion has carried," Ms. Ferringer said. She seemed amused, but Lily ignored that. She'd see how serious they were pretty soon. "I'm glad you're all so enthusiastic," she went on, "but I don't think you have to meet that often."

"We do if we're going to make a difference," Lily said.

She was glad to see Ian nodding his head, along with Suzy and Zooey, of course.

"Well," Ms. Ferringer said, "I've been told that the only thing the seventh-grade class has to do is a fund-raiser to buy something for the school. Y'know — like new soccer balls or some computer soft-ware."

Lily felt herself deflating again.

"I've got an idea," Ian said. He looked at Lily. "Is it okay if I have the floor?"

"What does *that* mean?" Zooey said.

"It means I can talk," Ian said.

Lily could hear Suzy whispering as she wrote, "Ian has the floor."

"I think we should poll our constituents," Ian said. He looked at Zooey, whose eyes were about to pop out. "Talk to the other seventh graders — find out what they want."

Zooey raised her hand.

"Yes?" Lily said.

"Do I have the floor now?" Zooey said.

"You do," Lily said. This was fun. She started to un-deflate.

"If we ask kids, aren't they gonna say stuff like, 'We want Domino's Pizza for lunch' or 'We want a longer summer vacation'?" Zooey said.

"Sure," Ian said. "But some people might actually have some real ideas."

Lily found herself staring at Ian. He hadn't said one dumb thing since they'd started the meeting. He hadn't even punched Lee on the arm or burped out loud.

"Does somebody want to move that?" she said.

She saw Ms. Ferringer stifle a giggle, but that was okay. Lily was on a roll.

"I so move," Ian said.

"Will anybody second?" Lily said.

The motion passed, and Lily told everyone to start polling right away.

Mr. Chester, their math teacher, was absent fifth period, and the substitute gave them a study hall. Lily took full advantage of the opportunity to do interviews.

Every person told her almost the same thing.

"I hate fund-raisers. Everybody in my neighborhood hides when they see me coming because I'm always selling something."

"This school stinks. I hate coming here."

"Who even worries about grades anymore — even in the accelerated classes?"

Lily had all of that running around in her head when she got to her locker after school that day. When Ian stepped up beside her, she didn't see him at first, and when she did, she jumped, knocking her geography book out of the locker and onto her foot. She waited for him to say she was a klutz. But he just leaned over and picked it up.

"You okay?" he said.

She nodded, too surprised to speak.

"I just wanted to say, I think we're gonna make a great team," he said.

"You do?" Lily said.

"Don't you?" Ian cocked one eyebrow up over his glasses frame.

"Oh, yeah, for sure!" Lily said. Her voice never stayed lost for long. "I've already done a bunch of polling, and everybody's way fed up with this place."

"Same here. And I think we can change some of that. You're a good president."

Then Ian smiled and walked away. Lily watched him until she couldn't see him anymore.

*This is gonna be so cool,* she thought when he'd disappeared. *I have to get Mom and Dad to let me do this. I have to!*

That night after supper, Mom and Dad sat down with Lily in the family room. Joe and Art had been asked to leave them alone, which made Lily's palms go clammy. When her parents cleared the room, they usually meant business.

But Lily had her own agenda, and she started right off with it.

"This isn't just another one of my new hobbies," she said the minute she hit the couch. "I know I haven't been very mature about my interests in the past, but this is different. I'm going to be very responsible about this, because me and the other officers — I mean, the other officers and me — are gonna really try to make a difference where it counts. What I really need from you guys is some help with those rule things for running a meeting. I already know it's what I'm supposed to be doing."

She took a big breath. Trying to sound as grown-up as Ian did was definitely hard.

"It's 'the other officers and I'," Dad said. "And I appreciate your seriousness about this." He stopped to take off his glasses and nibble a little on the earpiece. "But you still have an awful lot on your plate for a twelve-year-old girl."

Lily could feel her heart sinking. "Do you mean I have to give up being president? Even though I'm just getting started?"

"We're not robots, Lil," Mom said. "We're considering your feelings."

"Here's the plan," Dad said. He put his glasses on the table. Lily knew that five minutes later he'd be wondering where he put them. But his eyes weren't vague the way they often were. He focused them right on Lily — not necessarily a good sign. "Your mother and I want you to pray about all the things you're involved in and see if you can determine what things God really seems to want you to spend your time on."

"I've already done that," Lily said. "God says yes."

"Really?" Mom said. "How do you know?"

Lily shrugged. "It just feels right," she said.

Mom and Dad gave each other one of those I-know-what-you're-thinking looks.

"Feelings are definitely important," Dad said. He patted his pocket and then looked fuzzily around him. Lily picked up his glasses and handed them to him. "Feelings are important," he said, as he polished the glasses on the sleeve of his sweater, "but they aren't always our best indicator of God's will. The Lord gave you a brain, and it seems to me that's what you need to use in this situation."

"But I've thought about it!" Lily said.

"Have you thought about your spiritual gifts and whether you're using those for God?" Dad said.

Lily blinked at him. "What spiritual gifts? You mean like my lily cross Mudda gave me?" She fingered the cross from her grandmother that hung from a chain around her neck.

"Not that kind of gift, Lil," Mom said. "God's given everybody at least one gift that can be used to serve God's community. You know how some people are really great Sunday school teachers — "

"And some aren't," Lily put in.

26

"Exactly," Dad said. "You need to find out if leadership is a gift you have, or whether you ought to put your energies where your real gifts are."

"How am I gonna find out if I have a leadership gift if I don't try it?" Lily said.

Her parents looked at each other again. Dad even put on his glasses and squinted through the lenses, his eyes as blue and intense as Lily knew hers were at the moment.

"Let's do this," he said finally. "You continue to discuss this with God in your prayers, and in the meantime go ahead and be class president — "

"Yes!" Lily said. "Thank you!"

Dad put his hand up, and Lily clapped hers over her mouth. "But — if it appears at any time that this is not something you should do — that it isn't the best use of your gifts — you'll do the right thing and resign."

"And meanwhile," Mom said, "we will expect you to keep your grades up and do your chores and keep your quiet time."

Lily was bobbing her head with every item, but Dad said, "Maybe we ought to write all of this down in a contract. What have I done with my glasses?"

Mom's mouth twitched. "You're wearing them, hon," she said.

Lily posted the contract on her bulletin board in her room, and after she'd done her homework — and read from the book Dad had given her before she'd come upstairs, called *Robert's Rules of Order* — she started right in, writing to God about the gift of leadership and how she was sure she had it and how she was going to use it.

**Pick up a copy today at your local bookstore!**

Softcover 0-310-70250-X

27

## Own the entire collection of Lily fiction books by Nancy Rue!

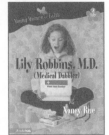

Here's Lily! (Book 1)
Softcover 0-310-23248-1
*The Beauty Book* companion

Lily Robbins, M.D. (Book 2)
Softcover 0-310-23249-X
*The Body Book* companion

Lily and the Creep (Book 3)
Softcover 0-310-23252-X
*The Buddy Book* companion

Lily's Ultimate Party (Book 4)
Softcover 0-310-23253-8
*The Best Bash Book* companion

Ask Lily (Book 5)
Softcover 0-310-23254-6
*The Blurry Rules Book* companion

Lily the Rebel (Book 6)
Softcover 0-310-23255-4
*The It's MY Life Book* companion

Lights, Action, Lily! (Book 7)
Softcover 0-310-70249-6
*The Creativity Book* companion

Lily Rules! (Book 8)
Softcover 0-310-70250-X
*The Uniquely Me Book* companion

*Available now at your local bookstore!*

Zonder**kidz**.

With this wonderful collection of non-fiction companion books, author Nancy Rue tackles everyday girl stuff from a biblical perspective!

**The Beauty Book ...**
**It's a God Thing!**
Softcover 0-310-70014-0
*Here's Lily!* companion

**The Body Book ...**
**It's a God Thing!**
Softcover 0-310-70015-9
*Lily Robbins, M.D.* companion

**The Buddy Book ...**
**It's a God Thing!**
Softcover 0-310-70064-7
*Lily and the Creep* companion

**The Best Bash Book ...**
**It's a God Thing!**
Softcover 0-310-70065-5
*Lily's Ultimate Party* companion

**The Blurry Rules Book ...**
**It's a God Thing!**
Softcover 0-310-70152-X
*Ask Lily* companion

**The It's MY Life Book ...**
**It's a God Thing!**
Softcover 0-310-70153-8
*Lily the Rebel* companion

**The Creativity Book ...**
**It's a God Thing!**
Softcover 0-310-70247-X
*Lights, Action, Lily!* companion

**The Uniquely Me Book ...**
**It's a God Thing!**
Softcover 0-310-70248-8
*Lily Rules!* companion

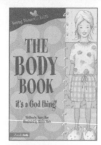
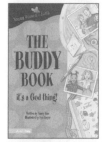

*Available now at your local bookstore!*
Zonder**kidz**.

# NIV Young Women of Faith Bible

## GENERAL EDITOR SUSIE SHELLENBERGER

Designed just for girls ages 8-12, the *NIV Young Women of Faith Bible* not only has a trendy, cool look, it's packed with fun to read in-text features that spark interest, provide insight, highlight key foundational portions of Scripture, and more. Discover how to apply God's word to your everyday life with the *NIV Young Women of Faith Bible*.

Hardcover 0-310-91394-2
Softcover 0-310-70278-X
Slate Leather–Look™ 0-310-70485-5
Periwinkle Leather–Look™ 0-310-70486-3

NEW!

NEW!

*Available now at your local bookstore!*

## Zonderkidz.

## More great books from the Young Women of Faith™ Library!

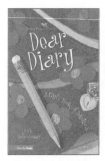   

**Dear Diary**
**A Girl's Book of Devotions**
Written by Susie Shellenberger
Softcover 0-310-70016-7

**Take It from Me**
**Straight Talk about Life from a**
**Teen Who's Been There**
Softcover 0-310-70316-6

**Girlz Want to Know**
**Answers to Real-Life Questions**
Written by Susie Shellenberger
Softcover 0-310-70045-0

**YWOF Journal: Hey! This Is Me**
Written by Connie Neal
Wire-O 0-310-70162-7

*Available now at your local bookstore!*

Zonder**kidz**.

# Now Available

## Rough & Rugged Lily (Book 9)
Softcover 0-310-70260-7

*The Year 'Round Holiday Book* companion

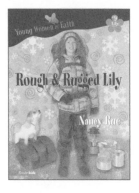

## Lily Speaks! (Book 10)
Softcover 0-310-70262-3

*The Values & Virtues Book* companion

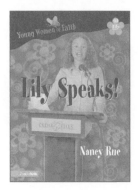

## The Year 'Round Holiday Book
## ... It's a God Thing!
Softcover 0-310-70256-9

*Rough & Rugged Lily* companion

## The Values & Virtues Book
## ... It's a God Thing!
Softcover 0-310-70257-7

*Lily Speaks!* companion

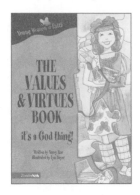

*Available now at your local bookstore!*

Zonder**kidz**.

We want to hear from you. Please send your comments about this
book to us in care of the address below. Thank you.

# Zonderkidz®

*Grand Rapids, MI 49530*
www.zonderkidz.com